IF I BE LIFTED UP

THOUGHTS ABOUT THE CROSS

IF I BE LIFTED UP

THOUGHTS ABOUT THE CROSS

By

SAMUEL M. SHOEMAKER, JR.

Rector of Calvary Church in New York
Author of "Children of the Second
Birth," "Twice-Born Min-
isters," etc.

Wipf & Stock
PUBLISHERS
Eugene, Oregon

Wipf and Stock Publishers
199 W 8th Ave, Suite 3
Eugene, OR 97401

If I Be Lifted Up
Thoughts About the Cross
By Shoemaker, Samuel M.
ISBN 13: 978-1-55635-192-1
ISBN 10: 1-55635-192-5
Publication date 1/16/2007
Previously published by Fleming H. Revell, 1931

To
H. S. S.

FOREWORD

LIVING religion is likely to begin in an individualistic experience. Through the help of another, or alone, we first discover the inner world of the Spirit, and its tremendous power in regulating and enhancing ordinary life.

Then as time goes on, we grow reflective about our experience. We find that others have been in the same places and known the same truths. By comparison and contrast we correct and enrich our own experience through historic perspective. We come to see the validity of much that we once thought was purely formal. We come to attach more and more importance to those eternal and absolute verities of the Christian religion, which are not dependent upon our own fluctuating and uncertain moods. We become interested in theology, almost in spite of ourselves: because most of us are intellectually curious, and want at least to be intellectually honest. Theology is only the attempt to think systematically about the things man believes and discovers about God.

This book is about the Cross. It is in no sense a complete theology of the Cross—not even as complete a theology as I believe in myself, and could write if there were the time. Such books are for students with leisure: a busy parish minister can only deal with these great subjects briefly, and as they touch the daily life of his people. These sermons represent an attempt to ap-

7

proach the central meaning of the Cross along several confessedly incomplete avenues of approach. I think of them as a little circle of converging, but incompleted radii, all pointing toward (and therefore in a sense defining), but none of them finally touching, the real heart of the meaning of the Cross. Were any of us able at last to do this, we should unlock the mystery of life itself. Even Dr. Moberly, in his great book *Atonement and Personality*, begins by saying: "Atonement is a reality much too fundamental to human consciousness, to be capable of any ready explanation. Our explanations, at their best, are still always partial explanations. It is always more than our understanding of it." And so it is that one does not hesitate to add his own convictions to the many words that are written and said about the meaning of the Cross of Christ.

I shall be happy if they can stir only a few people, as the thoughts and experience behind them have stirred me, to high moments of intense and amazed wonder at the Cross, to intellectual glimpses which even in their inadequacy have about them the feel of truth and reality, and to adventures in practical redemptive daring toward others, by which alone the great body of men, who know and care nothing for "theology" have it translated for them into the language of life.

S. M. S., JR.

Calvary Rectory,
  New York City,
    Epiphany, 1931.

CONTENTS

I

THE IRRESISTIBLE CROSS

"And I if I be lifted up from the earth will draw all men unto Me."—ST. JOHN 12: 32.

THOSE words come from a moment of great exaltation in our Lord's life, following upon a time of anxiety as He looked into the face of the Cross. There are spiritual exaltations which are not emotional reactions to depression, but which rather represent flashes of insight into reality. When He decided instead of praying to His Father to save Him from the Cross, to pray that His Father might be glorified by the Cross, a Voice spoke. Some thought it thundered and some that an angel had spoken. Jesus says that the Voice came not for His sake, but for those who heard it: and He sees the Prince of this world —the spirit of worldliness, I suppose we should say—expelled, while if He is lifted up on His Cross He will draw the world away after a new ideal of spiritual values.

Here is one of His stupendous claims. Imagine a Galilæan Carpenter saying that by His death on a criminal's cross He expects to transmute the world's values! But this is precisely what He claims. Now let us see for a little what He can possibly mean.

First let us remember that He is speaking in the realm of spiritual values, where no compulsion is known save the compulsion of the ideal itself. He does not mean by any means to coerce anyone into attachment to Him. He will " draw " them—attract them by the inherent greatness of His act, but not by taking any kind of advantage over them or forcing them. He is talking of the realm of men's spirits where arms and force are of no avail—where the willing homage of a man's heart is all that can possibly make any difference.

How then will the Cross draw all men?

This is not a theological but a practical question. The Cross was planted into the ground of a world where men are born to trouble as the sparks fly upward. And I think that the Cross will first draw all *suffering* men and women. There are distances in the scenery of the Cross where we cannot penetrate, but there are some things which lie upon its surface where the least intelligent, where even the least religious, can read. And one of them is that this loving Servant of the world chose willingly to suffer for other people, and made of His enforced pain a sacrament of blessing to others. If He be God, as we Christians think, then God suffered there on the Cross with man. We say, in a common but profound phrase, that " misery loves company "—it does because company alone can understand misery—and to have it fully understood is to divide it in half. They may be no theologians, but if I would understand the meaning of the suffering of the Cross I will go to some truly Christian invalid, or one who has long and bravely borne an inner sorrow—and they will tell me more by their lives than many a preacher by his words or arguments.

Again, the Cross will draw all *sinning* men and women who once catch sight of it. For there is something deep in human nature which responds to the necessity of sacrifice. When they used to catch a goat in Old Testament times, and figuratively bind their sins on his head, and turn him loose to forage for himself, naming him the scapegoat, they were groping after something. We cannot transfer our guilt to another, do what we will. But another may bear our guilt for us, bear it when we will not let it rest its weight upon our own shoulders: and that is just what a mother does who never gives up a lad who has gone wrong, but carries the shame of his life and bears him up in prayer so long as she lives. That kind of thing has an irresistible quality about it wherever you meet it face to face. It breaks men down into repentance when they think about it. Many a man down at Calvary Mission has carried with him wherever he has gone the picture of his mother grieving for him, carrying his sins for him. When God willingly stoops down, and upon a Cross where men can see,—a Cross which lends itself so easily to numberless representations in material, a Cross which it is so easy to remind oneself of by making the sign of it across one's breast —upon that Cross manifests His disapproval of sin, and His suffering for our sin, you have there a mighty deterrent to sin. There is something which defies full analysis here, as the Atonement itself defies full analysis: and yet is a fact which countless thousands have apprehended in their lives.

And I should say also that the Cross will prove irresistible to *thinking* men and women. When we begin to think at all, we find life a mixture of conflicting elements, and can scarcely say whether it is good or bad. Almost the first thing that a really thinking man or woman does is to rebel against the riddle of life. Very surely a riddle it is until you find an answer. Now it is not without significance that the human race has rescued from oblivion, and put Him at the head of our race, a Man Who died a failure on a Cross. That is an indisputable historic fact. Humanity has seen something significant in the Cross which it could not wholly explain, but to which it clung for dear life. Intelligent people will think about the Cross. For Christians, the Cross is the solution to the riddle. It is not a problem, it is an answer. And suffering love, bearing the burdens of others, remains life's last word. When the riddle is solved by that answer, and that answer is taken as a programme for life, the riddle disappears.

All of us, wise and foolish, great and small, suffer and sin and think. If the Cross can make its appeal to these, it will work its way in the world. Average humanity knows pain and sin, and knows that it needs the Cross. Intellectual humanity beginning at another place seeks finally the Cross, for solution there is none elsewhere. As the great Baron von Hugel says, " We are like children out in the night with one little candle." Christ is that candle, and the Cross is its brightest point. I for one am not afraid of the Cross being lost in a generation which is no longer much interested in theology. The Cross does not belong to theology, but to religion. And religion is a way of interpreting life in terms of a loving God. The Cross touches that problem at its highest and deepest point. And even if we wait for ages to accomplish it, Christ upon the Cross will draw the world to Himself. There He is saying something which we all understand. There He is doing something which, at our worst and our best moments we are also doing afar off—suffering and sacrificing. Because it has met a need in the human heart, the Cross will never disappear nor be supplanted. Here all of our life finds interpretation, and significance.

> Bane and blessing, pain and pleasure,
>   By the Cross are sanctified:
> Peace is there that knows no measure,
>   Joys that through all time abide.

It is usual for us to find Christ Himself first and the Cross later. May it please God that some of us, through our own crosses, should seek the great Cross, and finding Him Who used it for a throne, entrust to Him our lives for time and for eternity!

II

CHRISTMAS AND THE CROSS

"For verily He took not on Him the nature of angels; but He took on Him the seed of Abraham. Wherefore in all things it behoved Him to be made like unto His brethren, that He might be a merciful and faithful high priest in things pertaining to God, to make reconciliation for the sins of the people."—HEBREWS 2: 16, 17.

THERE was in the thought of the writer of this passage a connection between the Incarnation and the Atonement, between Christmas and the Cross. In them we begin with an emphasis upon His essential humanity, and are swept quickly to the emphasis upon His unique divinity as the world's Saviour. We travel in a moment from the homely events of Bethlehem, so readily understood by us all, even by our children, to the ineffable things that took place on Calvary.

I have thought that these words might come with a special meaning to us all on this Christmas Day.[1] We found on Thanksgiving that it was not possible simply to thank God for our own plenty: the day made us remember how many there were without life's bare necessities. Similarly to-day,

[1] 1930.

16

while we rejoice deeply in our hearts at the coming of Christ, we cannot but remember that this is for many a sad Christmas. Not only do many find themselves without what they have had in years gone by, but many feel the uncertainty of the winter ahead, as regards their work and their income. I have not seen so fine a Christmas suggestion as that of Will Rogers, that employers send their employes at Christmas a card which gives them the assurance that they will be continued in their positions. And then, I think, many of us are feeling the increasing power of the forces which are hostile to Christianity. There is pouring out of Russia a flood of anti-Christian propaganda. And here in our own land the trend of things is popularly away from faith rather than toward it. All of us feel the edges of the biting skepticism which is about us on all hands. It does not disturb the faith of any of us who know our Lord from experience: but it does make us realize that being a Christian to-day means something beside slipping easily along in serene and sunny faith, with no hardness to life and no suffering. Being a Christian involves a genuine clash with the world outside. We do not think the same thoughts, we do not believe the same truths, we do not stand for the same principles. There is an everlasting antagonism between Christian morals and the expediency of this world. I hope that the Church will never lose its touch with needy and sinful people, as Jesus never did. But we may as well face the fact now as later that the powers of this world found Him inconvenient and removed Him. And the disciples are not above their Lord.

And so let us take those verses and think about them a phrase at a time, for there is much meaning for us in them.

"Verily He took not on Him the nature of angels." The divine purpose of Jesus' coming into the world was revelation of the Father's love. Jesus might have been a celestial being, such as we call angels, and made that revelation perfectly clear. He could have been something between God and man, and revealed God to us. But He would always have appeared to the world, not as an angel, but as a phantom. Faith would then have been a subjective matter, to the minds of many. "But He took on Him the seed of Abraham." I want you to see the definiteness, the local-ness, the objectivity, the nationality of that. He was not only man, He was man with a lineal descent from other men. He made Himself part of a nation, of a tribe, of a family; of a country, of a province, of a town. Jesus thoroughly dug Himself in to our humanity, so that none might ever say that in anything He was separate from us.

Now once the writer has this humanity accepted, which is the heart of the Christmas message, he goes on to deal with the deeper meaning of the Incarnation. "Wherefore in all things it behoved Him to be made like unto His brethren." There was an inner and spiritual necessity for this utter and undifferentiated identity with human-kind, even to poverty, loneliness and temptation. And the necessity was " that He might be a merciful and faithful high priest in things pertaining to God." It was necessary that Jesus be our Brother before He should or could be our Saviour, that He should come to His work as Daysman between God and Man, saturated with the experience of being human. He could have stood between God and us, and interpreted God to us, if He had had the nature of an angel—but to be a " merciful and faithful high priest," He must know all that it means to be a man. *Then* His Cross " to make reconciliation for the sins of the people " is an experience which, on its human side at least, we can understand. In His body, in His feelings, in His pain on the Tree He represents you and me. The Cross is not a vision of the love of God let down once for purposes of human observation: but the Cross is a vision of the love of God through the love of a Man " in all things made like unto His brethren." Jesus' humanity, which is the note of Christmas, is the mirror of God's divinity, in the cradle, and in the Cross.

This means that the Cross is inherent in Christmas. Not alone is death inherent in birth for us all: but His unique death was inherent in His unique birth. We are all somewhat like children in our spiritual emotions, and we tend to be happy on Christmas, and sad on Good Friday, and happy again on Easter. It is well for us to feel acutely in ourselves those three contrasting significances. But no one of them can be seen apart from the other two, if it is fully to be understood. We have been already saying that the Cross takes its great meaning for us from Jesus' human closeness to us. We are now saying that Christmas takes its final meaning only in His Cross and His Resurrection. For the life of Jesus is " without seam, woven from the top throughout," like His coat at Calvary for which the soldiers cast lots. It is all one piece, for it is all one purpose. There are not tragic elements and joyous elements, moods of exaltation and moods of darkness, alternating in meaningless confusion: they come in a divine order, related one to the other. We shall never understand the Cross, except we understand Christmas: that Jesus is God come in the flesh. And we shall never understand Christmas, except we understand the Cross. The joys of Christmas are not the whole of the story. There is not only " peace on earth to men of good-will," but there is pain and sin on earth to men of ill-will. There is suffering to be assuaged, there is sin to be cleansed, there is guilt to be expiated. Thank God for a Christ Who deals with all of our humanity, all of our needs, and meets us in our darkness as well as in our joys!

And then, I think that there is a helpful progress from Christmas to the Cross, in following Jesus from the known into the unknown. The world as a whole has adopted Christmas. We understand it. It is very near us. We all have known, or seen in families near us, the joy of a little child coming into the world. Be it never so supernatural, nothing could be more natural than that God should come into the world in the same way as we all come. There is the intensely human side of Christmas. Why, in our gifts and presents, we can even in a faint way try to imitate it. Christmas is very close to us. But the Cross is not. The Resurrection is not. Our churches are full on Good Friday, because suffering is close to us, and Jesus suffered, and that is enough to draw us: yet few of us understand. Our churches are also full on Easter, when fashion decks itself and walks abroad: yet how many know the spiritual meaning of Easter? Think what it must have meant for the men who loved Jesus as a human being, were fascinated by His talk, by His way with children, by His unforgettable stories, who simply enjoyed His company, to hear Him say, " The Son of Man must suffer many things, and be rejected, and be killed." Think of how they winced and shivered and said, " Why are such things necessary? " They wondered why the preaching and healing in Galilee could not go on forever. They watched the gathering disciples. They saw the transformed lives. They felt the thrill of success, the dangerous thrill of spiritual success. It seems a strange fact that the deeper their fellowship grew with Him, the deeper grew the shadows about His life and theirs. As those bonds grew stout enough to stand it, every strain was put upon them to make them break. But they did not break, except one. The others stuck it out to the very end. And when their Lord returned to them again, they gladly served Him till the end came for them, and

for many it was martyrdom. Now Jesus asks us
to do precisely the same thing. He asks us to
begin with Him at the known and follow Him into
the unknown. He asks us to take all of Him that
we can understand in the evident manifestation of
Christmas, and move forward with Him into all
the experiences of life, unknown to us now whether
they shall be glad or sorrowful. There would be
no such thing as real faith if faith were sight, if
it were certainty of happiness, if it were insurance
against trouble. The disciples found Jesus trust-
worthy in the things that they could understand:
and in faith they followed Him where they could
not understand. He asks us to do that concerning
the theology of His religion. Begin where you
can. Say only that you believe God is like Jesus.
Or say only that you believe in Jesus' ideals—
start with the known and the understood. And
then in His company let your mind widen into the
fullness of faith. He asks us to do it concerning
our experience. You have begun to follow Him,
let us say; then the way grows suddenly hard.
You are tempted to say that faith makes no difference, or He has forsaken you. Not a bit of it.
You walked with Him where you could see: now
walk with Him where you cannot see, but He can
see. Remember His word to Simon Peter, " What
I do thou knowest not now, but thou shalt know
hereafter."

And then this relation between Christmas and
the Cross means that Christ is always coming into
our lives, whether by joy or by sorrow. There is

the quick, instinctive, happy faith of the shep-
herds, of Simeon and Anna, of the Wise Men, as
they see the infant Christ. And there is the faith
of loyalty which clings even when things are dark,
like Thomas saying, " Let us go also that we may
die with Him," or the faith that carried the women
and St. John and the Virgin to the foot of the
Cross. The faith that holds through the dark hour
is a much stronger faith, a much riper and maturer
faith, one much better gauged for the whole of
our life. It depends upon where and what we are,
how Christ comes to us. Sometimes we are enough
like children to have faith come in upon a wave of
joy, and we remember to be thankful. Sometimes
we are hard and self-sufficient, and nothing but
sorrow will ever reduce our pride and self-reliance,
and make us know how helpless we really are without God. One hopes and prays that this country
will be awakened by the difficulties of the present
time to realize that money is not everything, and
that God is as essential in a complex, comfortable
civilization as ever He was in simple and difficult
times. Some of you are just in the mood for
Christmas: you are happy and blessed and thankful, and God will come to you in that way. And
some of you are not in the mood for Christmas:
you are unhappy and sad and divided, and God
must come to you by way of the Cross. Either
way, do believe that God is knocking for an en-
trance into your life. If you can grasp it by joy,
then take it: but if you cannot, then look for it
in your trouble; it will be only a blessing in dis-

guise if God can use it as His indirect way of touching you, and causing you to seek Him just because you are so miserable without Him.

Dear people, we have got a wonderful Gospel. It is wonderful partly because it is so realistic about what is, and so idealistic about what might be. No airy nonsense about a spotlessly beautiful world: nothing is more severely realistic in facing the facts of suffering and sorrow and sin and death than Christianity. No cynical nonsense, either, about a hopeless world, incurable, incorrigible: nothing could be more idealistic than the Gospel about our human possibilities, once we realize fully our sonship to our Father in heaven. Christ is the measure of our hope. Christ Who shared our life to the dregs, Who knew it in its peace and in its pain, Christ of Christmas and of the Cross, is the beginning and the end of the Gospel. I can think of nothing which we need that is left out of Him or of His Gospel. Christmas is the day when all that treasure was given to us. And your joy this day will be exactly in proportion as you see with the eyes of faith what Christ really means about our life, about this world, and about the fundamental goodness of this universe.

God bless you all, and give to you a full measure of His abiding peace.

LORD JESUS CHRIST, Who didst lay aside Thy majesty and come amongst us as a little Child: Grant to us the grace to come to Thee as simply as Thou didst come to us. We thank Thee that in Thee God and man are forever made one. Send Thy peace to all who need it this day. Let Thy pity care for all who are alone and in need. Give us this year a deeper understanding of why Thou hast come to us, and what Thou art expecting of us. Let Thy peace hold our hearts, and let Thy love keep us this day from all unloving words or deeds. So help us to follow Thee in ways our fellows understand, as Thou didst reveal the Father to us in ways we could understand. We ask it in Thy Holy Name. Amen.

III

GOD'S ANTIDOTE TO PRIDE

"He humbled Himself."—PHILIPPIANS 2: 8.

TO look long ahead to an event spiritually commemorated is to increase greatly its value. There are many uses for Lent, but its great use for the spiritual imagination is to prepare the heart, through a long period of anticipation, for the overwhelming contrast between the utter blackness of Good Friday, and the blazing whiteness of Easter Day. Unless you feel and see the storm gather, you do not fully know why it bursts: and had there been no storm before it, the radiance of Resurrection would have been too much like any other sunny day. The reason why Easter Day is just a show-day for many lies precisely in the fact that they have not realized in their own quickened spiritual imagination the deep and divinely intended contrast between it and what preceded it.

I am going to consider with you to-day that quality in us which is the farthest of all from the Cross, and therefore needs spiritual treatment more than any of our moral ills, our pride. Jesus included it in the list of the things which come out of a man and defile the man. Those who made up the catalogue of the seven deadly sins put it where it belongs, at the head of the list. Pride is the deadliest sin of all. Of no other sins that I can recall is it specifically said in Scripture that God resists them: but of pride it is said twice in the New Testament, " God resisteth the proud."

Pride is " a high esteem of oneself for some real or imaginary merit or superiority." And let us have a look at some of the common forms pride takes. Pride is a kind of refined quintessence of everything that we mean by worldliness, and it is not surprising that in the very atmosphere wherein we live we breathe it in without even recognizing it. It blows about in the ether of our world, and it is terribly contagious.

I suppose the most rudimentary kind of pride, pride in its earliest stages, is pride like that of strong beasts—the pride of a big dog with a bone. He holds it between his paws in front of him where the little dogs can see it and smell it, but can't touch it. I am thinking of the kind of people who buy a lavishly expensive house and furnish it with the best that can be bought. I mean the kind of thing which goes beyond ordinary human comfort which can be said to minister to human efficiency: and which partakes unequivocally of the luxurious and the ostentatious. Those people say they have made their own money, and they want a house commensurate with their success: they will let stone and wood say in a mute but eloquent fashion that they have arrived. Or they say that it would not be fitting for people in their position of eco-

nomic superiority to move into a simpler neigh-
bourhood or surround themselves with simpler
things. Or a man with money says that the wish
of his life has been to give his wife everything
she can possibly desire: he wants to see her in a
setting of absolute comfort and beauty and refine-
ment. He has elaborate explanations for why he
does these things, but does it not all come back to
personal pride? When he sets foot in his vesti-
bule, and a great iron door swings open to admit
him into his hall, and he walks across deep, soft
carpet into his study, there is something in the
back of his mind which says to him, " *I* made what
bought this. *I* am the Master of this. *I* won that
lovely woman for my wife." And upon the feeling of superiority to somebody round the corner
which all this brings, his imagination feeds with
a never-satisfied hunger. He may call it success,
and position, and love: but at the base it is likely
to be pride—the pride of " a high esteem of oneself for some real or imagined merit or superiority."

There is a slightly subtler kind of pride, not
nouveau riche and upstart: more dignified and
better grounded than the first kind. It is the pride
of tradition, pride based upon what one's ances-
tors did, or one did oneself a long time ago. Tradition at its best seeks the preservation of what
was good in the past: but there is a kind of tradition which rests upon the laurels of the past, and
lives by putting a strain upon people's memory of
a long-forgotten day. I meet people every now

and then who give me the impression that they
have some special privilege within the Christian
church because their grandfather was a Bishop, or
they once had a cousin who was a missionary in
Timbuctoo. Or they dwell with great enthusiasm
on the place of their family in old New York—a
harmless and interesting reminiscence, which is
worth the keeping if it does not take up too much
room in the mind. But when this congeals, and
becomes a foe of progress; when, for instance, a
family cramps and badgers a boy into doing something he does not want or care to do because of
the tradition in his family, or because his name
goes with that kind of work, or he ought to follow
in his father's footsteps, there tradition has become
a form of slavery. There is, I am afraid, an amount
of not entirely concealed pride in the hearts of
many people who have been privileged with being
born into a family which has been known publicly
for a generation or two, which, without their knowing it, may become an actual enemy of religion.
People like that expect to be deferred to, not for
any moral or intellectual distinction in themselves;
but because they are descended from somebody
notable. Yes; they have within themselves, not
buried very deep, the pride of a " high esteem of
themselves for some real or imagined merit or
superiority."

But these first two are the least deadly forms
of pride. The pride of the man who glories in his
riches may have a naïve kind of humility mixed
with it: for his pride is in part a surprise that *he*

was able to make so much a success of himself.
It is a boyish kind of swelled-head, like that which
makes a seventeen-year-old too big for his boots
when he can thrash the boy across the fence. And
as for pride of ancestry and tradition, the world
of hard-work and simple origins looks on it with
a mixture of compassion and contempt. It is generally associated with old-mindedness, as boister-
ous pride in success is with a kind of immaturity.

But there are two forms of pride that are deadly
always and everywhere. The first is the pride of
intellect. The intellectual man has generally
worked his way through the silly and unsatisfy-
ing grounds for pride of the Go-getter or the Tra-
ditionalist. He is on much securer foundations.
He thinks that he is wholly rational. Very few in
society can gainsay him. The intellectual man has
attained a preëminence in our modern world which
gives him almost a hypnotic power over an age
that has more or less gone crazy over science and
knowledge. The casual unproved hypothesis of a
two-by-four scientist is listened to as law and gospel by crowds of people. Humanity is always looking for authority, and whatever can make itself
seem to speak with absoluteness, whether it be
church in one age or university in another, they
will listen eagerly to it, and swallow it whole. One
is grateful for all that thinking men have done to
clear the atmosphere of our present world; for
what they have done to rid us of fear and sick-
ness and inconvenience. But we shall have bought
these blessings dearly if with them has come a race

of haughty minds. We have heard a lot about the dogmatism of the theologian; but it is time somebody stood up and scored the dogmatism of the scientists too. I talked a little while ago with a great scientist, a humble scientist, Prof. Pupin, of Columbia. And he said quite frankly that science, like theology, often claims too much for itself and speaks with an authority it does not possess of matters it does not understand. I wish you could have heard him speak with enthusiasm of the other ways than purely intellectual of coming at the truth. It is never the great intellectuals one fears for; but pride fastens on the little fellows. And then they dogmatize like infallible popes! I think the intellectuals generally have heard about enough encomiums from Christian pulpits: it's time we parsons quit whitewashing a great deal of common pride masquerading as unbelief, and branded it for just what it is.

But the worst pride of all, deadlier far than any other, is spiritual pride. I dare to say that any man or woman is still full of pride who has not gone far enough in the Christian life to welcome any deeper spiritual challenge which implies that they stand now in spiritual need. The deepest realization we can have about ourselves is the realization that we are sinners. It is not a gloomy realization, far from it—unless you think that it is gloomy for sick people to want a doctor, or illiterate people to face the fact of their ignorance and want to learn. Being conscious of sin is just facing facts. And I find an appalling number of

Christian people who will say the General Confession, and say lustily in the Litany, " O God the
Father of heaven, have mercy upon us, miserable
sinners." But if you should say something which
arouses their conscience a bit, they will say outside, " Oh well, I'm not so bad—guess I'm about
as good as the next one." That is sometimes said
in fun; but it generally proceeds out of a heart
that has been dwelling upon its own superiority to
the rest of mankind; and that is not a very Christian kind of meditation.

And yet another very dangerous kind of spiritual pride, the pride of a reputation for spiritual
influence. I often wonder how some great preachers
have ever pulled through the amount of adulation
and flattery they have had from people who had
been helped, and who had heard of others that had
been helped, by the things they say. For a man
who deals much man-to-man there is a percentage
of failure which may keep him humble: but a
preacher who is only a preacher seldom hears of
a failure, it might do him more good if he did;
he hears of successes and people who have been
helped, helped in the things of God by the things
his own weak lips have said. And if he be fool
enough to put any trust in himself, to relax his hold
on God's power for one brief moment, he can
relapse into a pride strong enough to kill everything genuinely spiritual in his life. Anyone who
calls himself a Christian, and is beloved for human
service, is open to that temptation. Anyone who
has developed a reputation as a spiritual force is

bound to be subject to it more or less all the time. Plenty of men have drunk deep of spiritual success, and the wine has gone to their heads, and they have eaten out their last days in bitterness and sorrow because they succumbed to pride.

I need not go—there is not time to go—into other forms and phases of this thing. If any of us here to-day says he or she is free from it, they stand self-condemned as proud, and proven proud because they are satisfied. We all have regions and recesses in our minds where we carry about a tiny bit of pride, at the least; and a tiny bit of it is powerful, like a tiny bit of radium. It is the worst thing in us, worse than uncleanness, worse than irritability, worse than dishonesty. Our pride is on the other side of the world of our souls from God. God hates it, I believe God fears it, as nothing else in us; for it is the quickest, the most certain to cut us off from Him of all that comes between us.

This is the fact. What is the cure?

The antidote for pride is not humility, but gratitude. Humility is still struggling with one's own attitude: gratitude has found something without, in the presence of which to forget oneself and bow down in thankfulness. Pride may hide unseen in humility; but pride is gone out of thankfulness. Do you remember when the apostles came back from an evangelistic campaign, and Jesus was asking them about it; and in their enthusiasm of success, their pride of spiritual influence, they said, "Lord, even the demons are subject unto us through Thy Name." It was a danger signal, but Jesus did not say, " You must be humble." He said, " In this rejoice not that the demons are subject unto you: but rather rejoice that your names are written in heaven." Do not marvel at what God has done *through* you, for you may wind up merely marvelling at you: but marvel at what God has done *for* you, for He has had compassion on you and is saving you unto eternal life. The inspiration of His flashing answers to their revealed needs wants no further witness than its own inherent and self-luminous truth.

And what has God done for us? " He humbled Himself." He lived and died a Man. God found man in raging rebellion against Him: inflated with his freedom, drunk with his independence; insane with desire to have his own way. And first God thundered forth His commandments; and man did not listen. Then He cried aloud through His prophets; and man was stiff-necked in his self-will. You can't meet pride with anything that has force in it: they are too much alike. And then God died . . . died without the thunder of a single threat . . . died innocent and undefended on a Cross. And that was God's protest against man's pride. That was the way He " resisted the proud " —not by being proud Himself, but by cutting away all the foundations for pride, and laying the foundations for gratitude. Into the acid of man's pride He poured the alkali of His own condescending humility. And as a soft answer turneth away wrath, the humility of God turneth away the pride of man. And in His Cross He set up a principle by which, one glad day, all pride will be shrivelled into oblivion.

Oh, I know: we have all thought there were times when pride was desirable. We have said that we must keep our self-respect, as we have craved for our nations a place in the sun. But, my friends, I have never in my life let my pride help me out of a hole, where it would not have been better to depend upon some Christian quality. I have never called pride to my rescue where it would not have been better to call upon the Fatherly care and Providence of God; or to forget myself and appeal to a finer quality in someone who was trying to do me an injustice. Faith in God and in man will stand us in better stead than to look within and lean upon the uncertain staff of our own pride. I don't believe Jesus ever had anything to do with it, ever made the slightest use of it. He was tenacious of His message, He would not cast His pearls before swine: but " a high esteem of Himself for some real or imaginary merit of superiority " He never had. And I do not believe He wants us to have it. I have never seen it in the best of His servants, unless it were by way of lapse. We might, if God had never " humbled Himself " have been left wondering whether there might not be occasions when self-respect and pride were in order: but when He has died on the Cross? Never—not after that! He meant, if He meant anything by the Cross, to give all that He has and all that He is, for man. God, on a hilltop, in

Palestine, on our earth, died. Take that, and remember it, and think about it; and if before that Cross you can find room in your heart for one vestige of human pride, keep it,—for I can't. We are not our own, we are bought with a price; and the price was the most expensive thing God could think of, His own life. He is trying through that Cross to say something to you. If you know what it is you will be grateful, so grateful that every vestige of self-satisfaction will go out of you forever. He is hoping you will be so grateful you will never be proud again.

Our age has almost lost the sense of the deeper meaning of the Cross. We understand that by it God suffered with us, and entered into our life; but we do not understand that God suffered for us, and did something for us which has forever altered our eternal destiny. Our age has lost that deeper truth about the Cross primarily, I think, because we are so steeped in our pride that we have forgotten to recognize that we need saving. I wish that on this morning we might begin to behold afar off the Cross set up on Calvary's hill, and begin to make our journey toward that Cross by laying aside the greatest encumbrance which will hinder our way; and leave our pride, like the filthy garment that it is, by the roadside.

O GOD, Who hast given Thine Only Son for a witness of Thy love; and hast come to us in great humility and given Thy very Life for us: Help us to see ourselves in its light, and to put away from us the conceit and spiritual arrogance which blinds us to our need. And make us thankful for Thy mercy, and humble for Thy love. Through Jesus Christ our Lord. Amen.

IV

THE FEAR OF THE CROSS

"They did not understand what He said, and they were afraid to ask Him what He meant."—ST. MARK 9: 32 (Moffatt).

THIS is Passion Sunday, not the Sunday opening Holy Week, but the Sunday two weeks before Easter. The Cross has already risen on the horizon, and we are to ask ourselves concerning one of the meanings for us of that Sign which is " to the Jews a stumbling-block and to the Greeks foolishness, but to them which are called . . . Christ the power of God, and the wisdom of God."

The stony road from Galilee to Jerusalem, up hill and down dale, was not so far nor so long as the spiritual pathway from the sunny slopes about Nazareth and Gennesaret to the dark hill " outside the city wall." The two places represent two sides of Jesus' ministry, the ethical and the sacrificial. We would all prefer to spend our time with Him in Galilee, and listen to Him tell parables of the spiritual life, or watch Him heal the sick, or pray with Him up in the mountains. But modern Christianity is weak and anæmic partly because it has not faced Calvary, nor travelled down with Him

38

to Jerusalem, nor considered what it meant that
the climax of Christianity is manifested in the Best
Man the world ever saw lashed to a Cross.

Jesus Himself knew what would be the results
of speaking and living as He had been doing there
in the north. Scattered in amongst moral teach-
ings, to which no high-minded man can take excep-
tion, there are extravagant claims, dark sayings,
unique thoughts about His own centrality in the
world, which baffled men then and baffle them now.
He had certainly believed Himself the Messiah for
whom Judaism was waiting, and so had His followers. And that was well enough so long as He
said it off in the country, where the little local
courts, or Sanhedrins, could not deal with Him,
because blasphemy was not their province. But
the big Sanhedrin at Jerusalem had charge of such
cases. Any Jew knew that when a man had been
saying the things Jesus had been saying, if he
walked into Jerusalem, he walked into a trap.
Jesus knew how quickly a storm came up from
beyond the clear sky in Galilee: and He knew, too,
how all the popular clamour could turn to popular
rage. Three times in the earliest and simplest
account we have (St. Mark), does Jesus tell the
disciples frankly what awaits Him. The Son of
Man would be betrayed into the hands of men,
they would kill Him, and after three days He would
rise. He appears to have told them in the course
of their work, simply and unevasively. Jesus was
a realist. If the Cross was coming, they had better
face it and be ready for it. No use to accept

Simon Peter's unfounded and tempting cheerfulness, "Lord, be it far from Thee." Jesus knew in His soul that the Cross was inevitable. The only way to avoid it was to shirk His mission to mankind. So He set His face to go to Jerusalem.

But what did they do? Why, in spite of the times He had talked about it, they had managed to forget it. And when He mentioned it again, "they did not understand what He said, and they were afraid to ask Him what He meant." Already the Cross was to the Jews a stumbling-block. A Messiah who should teach first and reign afterwards,—that fell in with their visions. But a Messiah who should teach first and be crucified afterwards,—that was too grim to entertain for one moment in their minds. He was still young: why should He walk into the teeth of opposition and be killed? Why did He need to be killed at all? How would you have felt walking by His side, One Whom you loved better than life, while the roadway slipped by under your feet, and the distance to Jerusalem grew shorter and shorter, and He kept saying these awful things about dying? It was very natural to evade it as they did, and to let fear stand in the room of faith. There is no sharper contrast between Jesus and ourselves in the whole picture of Him than just here, where with perfect courage, candour and poise Jesus sees life steadily and sees it whole and death with it; while His human friends evade, ignore, explain away and fear to look the Cross in the face.

Oh my friends, how can anyone be so foolish

as to deny the reality of the Cross in our lives!
Only this week I have talked with a man whose
only child has died of a dread disease. It came
upon her unexpectedly after an early life of perfect health, and she died in fearful agony. Hour
by hour he sat beside her, suffering every pain with
her, till he told me that in his very body he felt
her physical pain. Tell a man like that there is
no cross in the world, no evil, no pain!—it is all
in our imagination, all a state of mind! He would
have good cause to throw you out of the house,
and say, " You stony-hearted idiot, you have never
suffered yourself, and you have no right to bring
your silly cheerfulness intruding upon real human
grief." The world is full to-day of self-hypno-
tized religion which seeks a cheerful spirit at the
expense of all other things, including the honest
facing of facts. Dean Inge says, " ' Whom the
Lord loveth He chasteneth.' A generation which
wishes for a religion without tears must find it
difficult to adjust its beliefs to the teaching of the
New Testament and the facts of life." No. These
people do not understand what Christ said, and
they are afraid to ask Him what He means. He
came to transfigure sorrow and interpret it, not to
tell us to ignore it for it does not exist. What
we need is not evasion, but interpretation.

The Cross is real; and because it is real men
fear it. What shall we do to rid ourselves of the
fear of the Cross in our own lives?

First, let us face it for a fact. Face the worst,
in reality and in possibility. Don't brood on it, but

face it. Are you afraid you have an incurable disease? Face it: get a thorough medical examination, be honest with yourself, and with those who have the right to know about you. Have you a dark spot of unbelief in your heart, so that your religion is a kind of wearing of a mask? Face it: admit it to yourself; remind yourself that it is not a final condition of mind, and expose yourself to searching religious experience, and to reading great books about religion. But don't fool yourself, be honest with yourself—and be especially honest as to the possible moral causes for unbelief in yourself, where sin hides faith from our eyes. Is there sin gnawing away at the vitals of your life? Face it: don't say you are not taking account of it, it's not a very big sin, you think it may wear off. Sin doesn't work that way. Look it in the face, and grapple with it, else you will carry it with you. Is your conscience pressing something upon you which you do not want to do? Face it: don't flinch and run away, for you cannot alter your deepest conviction, you can only obey it, or live a divided life. Has life laid upon you a narrow and circumscribed course, so that you have confining and sometimes irksome tasks to do for others? Again, face it: see just what is involved in it, and be honest about it with yourself. Jesus set His face to go to Jerusalem. He did not proceed to Jerusalem with His eye on Galilee, turning back, and wishing things were what they were not. He conquered because with open eyes He faced all the facts.

And then, He did something else. He took the

Cross voluntarily. For Him there was something else beside gathering human hostility which made the Cross inevitable. There was the love of God for the world to be made manifest where all men could see and could not forget: there was His own desire to offer Himself completely as the climax of His mission; there was an inward urge telling Him that nothing but His own death would break the heart of an indifferent world, and turn it God-ward. "Greater love hath no man than this, that a man lay down his life for his friends." He wanted us to know of this spontaneous element in the enforced Cross; and He told us that no man took His life from Him: He laid it down of Himself. Most of the unresolved human suffering that I have seen, the kind that burns and sears and ruins human life, is the kind which finds us at bay, fighting it, rebelling against it, refusing to accept it till it presses itself down like a chain about our necks, and we must suffer it dumbly and without the lift of willing acceptance and emerging significance. Make up your mind to accept the cross, the cross of duty at home, the cross of physical pain, the cross of being such a person as you are—and most of the bitterness of the cross is gone.

Third, let us set our cross in the light of a great purpose. From the immediate loss of His disciples, from the terrible details of the tragedy which confronted Him, surely our Lord Jesus Christ must have looked up into the heart of the Father again and again saying what is recorded in the twelfth chapter of St. John: "Now is my soul troubled; and what shall I say? Father, save me from this hour: but for this cause came I unto this hour. Father, glorify Thy Name." The Cross with a ring around it, isolating it from the process of God's redeeming love, taken all by itself, was then, and is now, unmitigated tragedy. But lifted up into that process, willed into being a part of it, "lo! it glows with peace and joy." And that is true of our little crosses, too. Our lives are items in God's whole plan, words in the great book He is writing, soldiers in His great cosmic warfare. What if we suffer in the campaign? It is the Cause that matters: and we only matter because we matter to the Cause. So it is that, as the Baron von Hugel says, "pain gets fully faced and willed, gets taken up into the conscious life. Suffering thus becomes the highest form of action, a divinely potent means of satisfaction, recovery and enlargement for the soul,—the soul with its mysteriously great consciousness of pettiness and sin, and its immense capacity for joy in self-donation."

Fourth, let our cross give us larger hearts and deeper sympathies. Trouble always turns us in, or turns us out. We either feel sorry for ourselves, or we feel sorry for all the rest of mankind. Trouble is a kind of sacrament: and God means it to work a work of grace in us, and then to open our hearts to all human needs. You have heard this before, and there is nothing new in it: but maybe the *experience* would be new if it came and transfigured your trouble into sympathy. How often do sick people force their little world to revolve about them, for once in their lives getting their way, and being spoiled like children because this is not the time to enforce discipline. Yet I have seen one lately, in real danger and great pain, sending messages to others, keeping them in mind, praying for them, and keeping the center of life in Christ and in other people, not in that sick-room. As I talked with that man who had lost his child, he said bravely and with ringing faith, " Surely there must be a meaning in all this for me." And we soon agreed that it probably lay in the enlarging of his heart toward that which all men suffer. God forbid that we suffer, and then come out just what we always were, or reduced to the depths of self-pity and self-concern!

Finally, let us see in the Cross the sign of the new success. I shall never forget reading for the first time a sentence from Dr. Orchard which has remained with me ever since: " When a man accepts Christ he must do so upon the absolute basis that Christ is what he means by truth, and His career is what he calls success." *His* career is what we must call success! Not fame nor money nor ease nor prosperity nor great accomplishment— but Jesus as the measure of success—Jesus, all of Whose life was tinged with the Cross where He came to its climax. The Cross as the sign of success! Yes: he that has been admitted into that blessed secret has gone where the world can no longer delude or entrap him. That man alone in all the world is *safe*. As Browning says,

Measure thy life by loss instead of gain;
  Not by the wine drunk, but by the wine poured forth;
For love's strength standeth in love's sacrifice;
  And whoso suffers most, hath most to give.

Sometimes when I see a life take flight from home
to go to the ends of the earth for the Lord Jesus
Christ, having turned his or her back upon most
of what we consider as success I say to myself,
" There is one who belongs to the apostolic suc-
cession of the sacrificers. There is one who has
earned the privilege of suffering, and who is initiated as only such an one can be into the mystery
and the certainty of the success of the Cross."

Christianity is many things. It is a philosophy
of life. It is a way to make a new world. It is a
life of supreme adventure and profound joy. We
need to remind ourselves that it is also the message of a consecrated cross to bear. We love the
serene and Galilee-parts of the Gospel—the graciousness and poetry and infinite tenderness and
humanity of Jesus. But we are repelled by the
grim and Jerusalem-parts of it—the blood and the
hate and the sacrifice. *We have a crucified Saviour.* If we can't stand it, if we want a smiling,
victorious, successful Christ, as many moderns try
to make Him to be, we must make a Christ for
ourselves—for the One in the Gospels is not after
this fashion. If, like those apprehensive apostles
of old, we " do not understand what He says, and
are afraid to ask Him what He means," if we seek
a Gospel without one great atoning Cross of

Christ, and a million daily crosses for the million of us to take up and carry for Him, then in literal truth we "cannot be His disciples." The only Gospel for this kind of a world is a Gospel which reckons with sin and suffering and evil, and gathers them up into its own whole significance.

But the Christ Who lays the cross upon us, and commands us to carry it, He alone consecrates and transfigures that Cross. The fear of the Cross gives way to faith, and even to joy. Old Jacob Böehme, one of the great seventeenth-century mystics, said, "Life is a strange bath of thorns and thistles" : yet he went through the world, "having a joy in his heart which made his whole being tremble and his soul triumph as if it were in God." Christ alone Who bore and transfigured His own Cross can teach us the secret of bearing and transfiguring ours.

And when one day the Cross appears upon our own horizon, when in our service for Christ we are at last allowed the privilege of sharing in the fellowship of His sufferings, let us not misunderstand what He says through an attempt to evade the reality of the Cross, and let us not fear to ask Him what He means by it for us. But remembering His Cross, let us make every cross the death of self, and the gateway to a new life.

O LORD JESUS CHRIST, help us to be willing to face our crosses. Take from us all fear, and lead us through suffering to deeper joy and larger sacrifice. For Thy Name's sake. Amen.

V

WHO CRUCIFIED CHRIST?

". . . they crucified Him."—St. Luke 23: 33.

AS we remember the Triumphal Entry of Jesus into Jerusalem and realize, as none but He did on that first Palm Sunday, what awaited Him but a few days off, let us think of who crucified Christ. The stories as told in all four Gospels are completer than those concerning any other event in His life, so that we shall be moving upon solid ground with no need of further imagination than that which is required to put ourselves in the presence of unquestioned facts. There must have been some reason why all the forces of His time rose up unitedly to put to death that Life which later ages have come to recognize as the greatest Life that ever graced our world. Let us consider the human factors which caused the crucifixion.

The first who come to our mind were the Pharisees. They were the religious leaders and enthusiasts of the time. To them the Law was the way to serve God, and they observed it with that meticulous and irrational completeness which is known to us all from our Lord's criticisms of them. They believed in the immortality of the soul, and expected the Messiah. But they are chiefly known

48

in New Testament times by their spiritual exclusiveness. In public they would worship with the common people, and they shared their beliefs. But when worship was done, they gathered their skirts about them and withdrew into their own conscious superiority and exclusiveness. These were the clergy and the church-people of the time. Better than they there were not: in them religion reached its pitch and zenith. They were guardians of the faith, purists in morals. Certainly not all of them were hypocrites and insincere: some of them changed and followed Christ. But it is an appalling thought that the first men who come to our minds as the crucifiers of Christ were the acknowledged religious leaders of the day. He made too many claims for them and that scandalized their theology: and then He fortified those claims by what He did for broken and sinning humanity, things which they could not do. For the purity of their theology, and for the safety of their institution, they voted for His crucifixion.

In Pilate you find the incarnation of imperialistic government. A procurator in Palestine must watch both the capital and the province. His function was to keep taxes flowing back to Rome, and to keep the province quiet. In Palestine he must be ingenious in that way which Rome seems to have discovered, and which Great Britain certainly follows to-day, the way of wise compromise, not stinging the subjects to violence by unreasonable demands, but playing up to their beliefs and accommodating itself to their customs. Pilate needed to be popular in Palestine, or somebody would complain to Rome. And here is a Nobody from Galilee—a religious crank, a Man to excite the people and stir up religious fires, and indirectly political unrest. Because He amounted to nothing, and had not a prominent citizen on His side, the first and only consideration for Pilate was the politically shrewd thing to do. Justice never has been quite so free to poor men as to those fortified with wealth or rank. For the smooth-running of his government, for the continuation of his own governorship, Pilate voted for crucifixion.

Then there were the Sadducees. Somewhat incidentally they were religious men, but primarily they were the conservative business men of their time. They looked back to " the good old days," were chary of reform, believed in the *status quo*, and had a mind to their pockets. They had no belief in immortality and this seems to have heightened in them the sense of the importance of this world and what one could squeeze out of it. These were men of sense, of judgment, of business acumen. They were people you would consult about your investments and your real estate, and you would not be led astray. If Jesus had been content to stay up in Galilee, in the up-country regions where a little sedition and radicalism would do no harm, they would never have disturbed Him. But when Jesus invaded the Temple and began to make a commotion about perfectly legitimate ecclesiastical business, that was too much. And the Sadducees believing that a dead radical was the only

safe radical, in order to preserve the order of
human society under which they lived, voted for
the crucifixion.

Herod was a native ruler in the north country
who by favours had been won over to work for
Rome against his own people—a quite parallel
situation to many of the native princes of India
to-day in their relation to England; and if we
Americans have not done the same thing, it is
probably from want of the chance, or perhaps we
have done it through economic rather than political favours. Herod was a buffoon, and a profli-
gate. Jesus had no use for him: " beware of the
leaven of Herod," He said, and in another place
He called him " that fox," seeming to imply a sly
character for which He had contempt. Jesus, as
He stood there before Herod, must have made him
think of the old prophets of the land, of Judaism's
strong and rugged past and great spiritual hopes,
of all the things on which Herod had turned his
back. Jesus might have been an incarnation of
whatever remains of conscience Herod had. So
Herod began to ply Him with questions, questions
to take up time rather than to find out anything,
questions to stifle the truth rather than to discover
it. Jesus said nothing. And all that this royal
clown could think of was to dress his victim in fine
robes, in mockery for His divine claim, and pack
Him off to Pilate. Herod voted for the crucifixion
because he was already so compromised he could
do nothing else: the larger factors in the case could
not weigh with him. To send Jesus back to Pilate

with no comment from His own countryman would
strengthen Herod's position with Rome—and that
came first.

So far we have been considering those who were
so prejudiced against Jesus that they could hardly
be open-minded. They were His enemies from the
start. But now we come to one who was His
friend, and who by his friendship for Jesus set in
motion the machinery of the crucifixion. Judas is
a difficult character to analyze, because he is a
character which is complex. Something in him
drew him to Jesus, and something in him kept
drawing him to the devil. Many feel that he was
a disappointed idealist, that he joined up with the
company of Christ for some hope of reform or
political liberty: but as time went on it became
clearer and clearer that Jesus' kingdom was not
of this world, that He was not set upon particular
reforms, but upon the regeneration of individuals
and indirectly of society. He was carrying it all
too far for Judas, who saw no need for risking
crucifixion by flying into the face of public opinion
in Jerusalem. I sometimes think that Judas' betrayal developed out of nothing more at the beginning than a difference in method: but that grew
into disagreement, and that into disillusionment,
and that into disloyalty. And it was His own
familiar friend who led His captors straight to
Him in the garden, and made the crucifixion inevitable.

At the other end of the Crucifixion story were
another group implicated in Jesus' destruction,

though as minor agents: and those were the soldiers of Rome. I suppose that crucifixion was not altogether uncommon to them, for it was the common means of execution in that day. They were part of a system. They were nearer to *things* than men anywhere else can become. They were the last dreadful link in a complicated chain of causes, and I doubt if they felt themselves any wise at fault. The military machine in every generation is the most powerful force to take the moral sensitiveness out of a man. Said a Russian soldier in the Great War, "Now I fear neither God nor the devil. After I had stuck a bayonet into a man's stomach, it was as if something had fallen away from me." I suppose that something had literally "fallen away" from those men during their days of soldiering: and the continuous petty discipline exercised toward subject people was even more demoralizing than fighting: the cruelest, most brutal soldiers I ever saw were the Japanese soldiers in Korea in 1919, where the situation was quite similar to that of Roman soldiers in Palestine. If you say that soldiers cannot have their own personal responsibility because they are men under authority, I say that no man has any business ever to allow himself to be in a position where his own moral autonomy is taken away. Any occupation which allows you to be an unconscious agent in a tragedy like Calvary is no occupation for you to be engaged in!

Yet one more group must we consider. And that is the public. Even in a subject country, they ex-

ercise their pressure. There are points past which
no wise ruler will go, for a populace lashed to fury
can cause considerable trouble. We all make up
public opinion, by the level of our lives and by
the talk of our lips. Into the highways they came
pouring to see what was happening. The Prophet
of Galilee had come to town and gotten into trouble: they would come out and see what was to
happen. They had no responsibility for Him.
They may have felt sympathy and pity for Him,
or they may have said, " He had better have left
well enough alone." But in any case they did
nothing. They were unorganized, but somebody
might have organized them at once, and filed a
complaint and pled for better justice. They might
have done something besides stare, if only one of
them had had any courage. To most of them it
was all just a piece of excitement. They looked
upon it as the crowds in a subway read of a man
murdering his children, while they chew their gum
and turn over the page. The crowd voted for the
crucifixion because some of them wanted to please
Pilate and the rest of them hadn't the courage to
do anything.

Now, my friends, I want to ask you how far a
jump it is from the world which crucified Christ to
our world. Have you seen no parallels thus far?
Do you think these old motives are cleaned out of
our society, or even out of our hearts? We must
ask ourselves what is still being done to the heart
of Christ if He still feels as He did, and we still
act as they did.

Do our church-people, and our leaders, the
Bishops and clergy, live and act and decide in the
spirit of Christ, or the spirit of the Pharisees? Are
we on the whole more interested in simon-pure religion of the Spirit, or in the maintenance of the
religious institution? I do not ask that question
captiously but sincerely, for I wonder what our
Lord thinks about us as He looks down on us. I
see our leaders breaking their backs over institu-
tional budgets, saddling themselves with a mass of
machinery and organization, camping in the offices
of rich men to get their debts paid: these things
may seem important, but they steal time from
those more important fields, the enrichment of the
inner life, and the living contact with needy souls,
which is the function of the prophet. We do not
produce prophets to-day, and we do not like them
when they appear. When I realize what the Epis-
copal Church did to Bishop Paul Jones in the war,
because he set out to take our Lord's commands
about war literally, I hang my head in shame, and
I know that there are too many within our ranks
who do not care to have the disturbing questions
of the prophet levelled at our personal, social, religious or national life. Christ usually comes, as
He came at first, in an unexpected guise. You do
not find Him so much in the officials and great
ecclesiastical pronouncements, as in the inspired
nobody who generally is the human agent of spiritual awakening. A great Christian Jew said to
me some years ago that but for an experience of
Christ which he could not go back upon, he would

go back to Judaism, for the Pharisees are in the Christian Church.

When it comes to politics, because we happen not to be an imperialistically-minded people, we are apt to look for the modern sin of political expediency in other nations, and to think that we see Pilate ruling still somewhere across the sea. But there are a good many things our government ought to do if it had the courage. It ought to look thoroughly into our treatment of the Japanese on the west coast, and see whether the seeds of war are being sown by race prejudice and arrogance on the part of our people. It ought to look into the situation of the coal-miners, and study the question of unemployment with a good deal more concern than one can normally expect from the government of a rich country. And in my judgment it ought to stop quibbling about fine points and line up with the forward-thinking opinion of the world in a federation which will make war an impossibility. We are found guilty of political expediency, which still crucifies Christ in His little ones, rather in the things we leave undone than in the things which we do. Our country can afford, if any can, to take and maintain a consistently generous and idealistic spirit. Are we doing it? " Inasmuch as ye did it not unto one of the least of these—ye did it not unto Me."

And the Sadducees with their economic conservatism, the pillars of business, the defenders of the *status quo*. We produce people like that by so many thousands here in New York that to mention them is almost enough. You will find them in down-town offices, and you will see their shiny heads through a very large window pane in the clubs on Fifth Avenue; many of them kind, church-going men. But you know that they feel themselves quite consciously superior, an aristocracy not of social position, which is amusing and harmless, but of economic privilege and divine right which is dangerous. When they can worship Jesus from a distance, with stained glass windows about to keep off the too-clear light of realities, they will do it. But they do not want to hear much about His sociology or His views as to wealth. How do these nice old men crucify Christ? By poor wages, by lack of understanding, by keeping up a system which maims and reduces vast numbers of individuals and families to a standard below what can support life. You say, What shall we do? The first thing to do is to admit we are dissatisfied with a society which cannot by any stretch be called Christian. We must get a spirit of dissatisfaction first: and that the Sadducees resent.

Herod typifies the modern spirit of self-indulgence and irresponsibility. And that judgment lands on us all. Very few of us there are who do not live up to our means, advancing our standards of comfort beyond reasonable needs, and travelling and pampering ourselves when we have the mind. There are very few disciplined people to-day. Frowning at the stern harshness of Puritanism, we have forgotten that in character a touch of Puritanism will always be needed if we are not to grow soft and deteriorate. One of the greatest needs of our time is a religion which will again introduce the deliberately hard note of discipline to counteract the Herodian love of ease and pleasure. If you don't believe that kind of thing crucifies Christ, go and see how much of Christ you can find in lives like that. They crucify Him by preoccupation with other things.

In Judas I see the man who gives up his faith. A man told me this week that he became a Christian, and then went back on it, and was now an atheist, because of the hypocrisy of other Christians. I had to tell him that while I did not condone the hypocrisy of other Christians, I did not think God would ask him any questions about other people's hypocrisy. Floating about in our world are thousands of men and women who for some small reason,—a minister they didn't like, a church where they found a cool reception, a theological point they had not settled,—have pushed the whole business of religion overboard, and by the satisfaction of their own independence betrayed Christ and the best that was in them. You are in league with something in our modern world: if it is not God and the right, it is apt to be the world and the wrong, for not many of us remain detached and wholly alone. By your absence from His house, by your failure to support His work, by your failure in growth and freshness in your spiritual life, you crucify Him afresh.

The soldiers stand for something else besides

the military only. God knows Christ is always
crucified by militarism and by war, which, however kindly he may be personally, is the soldier's
business. But these soldiers stand for all men
caught in a web of their own making, so that they
are not free to serve God with abandon. That
web may be your home, or it may be your business, or it may be your anxiety, or it may be your
very conscience: it makes for rigidity within you,
unwillingness to remake your plans, to change your
ways, to trust God if He calls you to something
higher. Christ is crucified by our stunted goodness as well as by our wickedness. Whenever the
possible best in any situation is not attained, Christ
is crucified. We sometimes kill Christ by not being willing to be something else besides what we
are.

And then the mob-spirit. Do you think Jesus
is far away when black men are lynched by white
men in our own south-land, or that His own flesh
does not quiver in that fire? Do we go to war
because we know the facts and believe in the ends
of that war, or because we have read the news-
papers and caught the fever and are drawn along
by government propaganda and the cries of the
crowd? And as the mob-spirit can be active where
it should not, it can be inactive where it should
not be: public apathy is often as wrong as public
hysteria. We still crucify Christ by what we do
not do. We could stop war, and race prejudice,
and even poverty if we had the mind, and some
leader would champion the cause and band us with

him. But would we go, or would we hang out of the windows watching Christ go by to crucifixion, rather than troubling to go out and say a word of protest?

I have said enough. We belong to that kind of a world. These people are not remote Jews and Romans, they are modern Americans, our friends, our relatives, our associates. The poisons which were at work in first century Palestine are still at work in twentieth century America. You and I are both the products and the creators of such a world. It is a world which murders Christ and His little ones who like Him are unprotected. Do you feel shame for it? How much shame do you feel? While in our churches He has His Palm-Sunday ovations, Good Friday waits for Him in the world without. This world crucified the Lord of Glory. His death atoned for our sins. Did you ever think that our life ought somehow to atone for His death—that some way all this repeated crucifixion ought to stop, that your life and mine should be at His disposal to stop it?

God help us not to go unthinking through this Holy Week, laying the blame for Christ's death upon other men. The text is " they crucified Him." The truth is also " we crucified Him." And when we seek to fix the guilt, let us all ask the question, " Lord, is it I? "

OUR MASTER AND OUR FRIEND, Who didst suffer for our offences, Show us where in our own lives we are crucifying Thee afresh to-day. Bring us face to face again with the scene of Thy victory and Thy defeat, and show us whether we are really Thy friends or Thine enemies. May our selves be crucified with Thee in this week, and bring us to an Easter of New Life through the death of our self-will. We ask it for Thy merits, Whom with the Father and the Holy Spirit we worship as one God world without end. Amen.

VI

PILATE AND THE CRUCIFIXION

"What then shall I do with Jesus which is called Christ?"
—St. Matt. 27: 22.

THE province of Palestine had cost Rome more than ever it was worth. The quality in the Jews which has made them unassimilable by any people amongst whom they have lived, made them also psychologically unconquerable by any people who happened to win a war with them. And so it was that Rome appointed, in A. D. 26, a procurator about whose courage and despatch there was no question, and who had in him a fair share of Roman action. His name was Pontius Pilate: and he had needed all the acumen he had to deal with the insurrections and mutinies of the Jews, who were not averse to going behind him and reporting his cruelties and corruptions to the Emperor at Rome. Every record, sacred and secular, tells the same story of complete exasperation with each other on the part of Pilate and the Jews.

And so when Jesus comes up for trial, there is much more to be considered than immediate justice.

The Sanhedrin could only meet by day, and

their formal charge could only have been made after dawn: but the real trial had been held during the night. It was not easy to get this business done. They might employ two false witnesses to swear a charge against Jesus: but there were decent men in the Sanhedrin, men like Nicodemus and Joseph of Arimathæa, who must be reckoned with. Two men finally came forward to say that Jesus had declared He could destroy the temple of God and build it in three days. The High Priest asked Him what He had to say: and Jesus made no reply. Then of his own motion the High Priest adjured Him by the living God to say whether He was Christ, the Son of God. Concerning His own safety Jesus would make no comment: but concerning the truth for which He lived, He would proclaim it everywhere. " Even so! ", He said, " and you will see the Son of man seated at the right hand of power, and coming on the clouds of heaven." That was enough. It was blasphemy, and the crowd concurred that He was doomed to death.

Now the power of life and death lay not in the Sanhedrin, but in the procurator. Picture Jesus, then, that Passover morning, led through the streets to the Prætorium, into which His captors could not enter because of ceremonial defilement. Pilate comes out in deference to their scruples.

You will remember the chief factors in the story: Pilate asks the Jews for a charge, and they say that if He were not a criminal they would not have brought Him. Pilate tells them to take Him and judge Him according to their law, and the fawning Jews say they have not the power. Then Pilate calls Jesus in alone, and asks whether He is the King of the Jews. Jesus' answer is a question: "Are you saying this of your own accord, or did other people tell you about me? . . . My kingdom is not of this world—you do not understand." "So then you *are* a King?" says Pilate. And Jesus says His is a kingship of truth—and how it must have galled that shifty compromiser to hear it!—who replied, as he was going outside, "What is truth!" Then came the choice of Barabbas to go free while Jesus went bound. Pilate scourged Jesus to appease the Jewish thirst for punishment of Him, little realizing that hatred is not satisfied but only inflamed by cruelty. "I find no fault in Him" is Pilate's verdict. But the Jews cried for His crucifixion, and said that by their law He ought to die, for He had made Himself God's Son. Again Pilate took Jesus inside, and questioned Him, and came out trying to release Him. But the people said if he did, he was no friend of Cæsar's. When last he brought Him out they cried again, "Crucify Him." And, the story closes, "their voices prevailed," and Pilate handed Him over to them to be crucified.

Let us look more closely into what the elements were which caused this final feeble permission which can hardly be dignified as a decision.

On the positive side, Pilate had nothing personally against Jesus. Without question he was impressed by Him, and four times sought in a weak-

kneed fashion to release Him. " I find no fault
in Him " we may take as meaning something more
than a failure to discover just cause for His execution. I think Jesus *interested* Pilate. To these
factors was added also superstition: while he sat
on his bench, word was brought to him from his
wife, saying that she had dreamed about this Man,
and Pilate had better have nothing to do with Him.
Whether this was pure superstition, or whether it
was a woman's intuition or a wife's acute concern
for her husband's position, makes no difference: it
must have given Pilate a terrible twist in his soul
when he got the message. Then there must have
been a touch of mercy in the heart of the most
iron Roman, and Pilate could not but be moved
by the simple sincerity of this Man. And there
was surely some sense of justice in him which made
him feel the unfairness of this whole procedure.
And there was even something spiritually wistful
in the question " Whence art Thou? ": Pilate had
had a pagan upbringing, with teaching about gods
who sometimes came to earth: what if his childish
faith were better than he thought, and here stood
one of them? I think Jesus *frightened* Pilate. All
these considerations would have made for letting
Him go.

But there was all the other side to be thought of.
Jesus could be considered insubordinate if Pilate
wanted to construe His silence so: the Roman was
in character when he said, " Knowest Thou not
that I have power to crucify Thee and power to release Thee? " Then he had had enough Jewish in-

surrections in the six years of his office, and he did
not want to rouse them to fresh dissatisfaction: so
that immediate popularity must be considered.
The mob of people without was stirred with anger,
and was ready enough to make things difficult for
Pilate by going to Tiberius again: so that slightly
more remote political expediency must be considered. He might be recalled, and he might be reduced. Jesus could not answer directly that question about being a king, for had He said yes, it
would have meant something to Pilate which He
did not intend: and the acceptance of the name,
with all that it might imply of a secret society—
and they were the bane of a ruler's existence—
was enough for a handle by which to condemn
Him. A religious danger to the Jews was nothing
to him—the more they were occupied with religion
the less they would be occupied with politics. But
a possible political danger to Rome, or the excuse
to imagine one, was another matter.

What Pilate tried to do was to steer between
these two conflicting positions by action which was
so neutral and evasive as hardly to be action at all.
First he pushed the responsibility from him, the-
atrically washing his hands. Then he tried to dis-
tract the attention of the crowd by a new plaything, a reminder of the excitement of releasing
a prisoner to their wishes at the feast, and offering them the choice between Jesus and Barabbas
—but they chose Barabbas. Then he scourged
Jesus as a sop to the popular desire for some kind
of revenge. Weakly he protested Jesus' innocence

and his own. " See ye to it," he said, which he
could not define more precisely by telling exactly
what he meant. Finally, as if to put the matter
entirely outside his own control by infuriating the
Jews, he brought Jesus forth into the Pavement,
and said to them, " This is your King! " And so
loud was their fury that Pilate let it be also his
judgment: and so Jesus was crucified.

In all this welter of confused emotion and desire, what stand out as the major characteristics
of Pilate? I should say they were three: *self-interest, wistfulness,* and *cynicism*. No matter what
went by the board or who suffered, Pilate would
keep his place: he was not going to be driven back
to Rome by the complaints of these despicable
Jews; and loathe them as he might, he would play
them for what they were worth to him, and keep
them appeased. Pilate would take care of himself.
But there seems to me to be a window into a soul
at base religious in his question of Jesus, " Whence
art Thou? " " Where do you come from? " The
thought may have been started in his mind by
Jesus' declaration that His kingdom did not belong
to this world: but whatever its origin, it is a
religious question, or certainly one tinged with religious feeling. Jesus must have seen in Pilate this
superstition bordering on wistfulness: and how He
could have played upon it if He would; what could
He not have said of terrifying truth about sin and
judgment, His grave eyes beating down on Pilate
till he broke into a sweat! But no—He left that
wistfulness to grow: and no wonder that amid the

legends of his fearful end, there is another that
Pilate later became a Christian. But it was a
strangled, thwarted wistfulness, lying in the back
of his mind. In the front of his mind was cynicism. It better comports with worldlings and politicians. " What is truth! " was his creed: the
higher life was an emotion for women and children; religion and ideals and spiritual aspiration
were visionary and unreal. What counted was
action and cash and common sense in the immediate. Now I believe that it was the conflict between these two natures in him, the smothered love
for the ideal, and the long-trained love for the
expedient, which gave him the incapacity for an
inner decision which is characteristic of the cynic.
If there had been nothing but a trial of a criminal,
he could have got through it well: but *this* Criminal touched his conscience, his mercy, his justice,
his buried soul. He was utterly over his depth.
This was a new world. The Ideal had suddenly
come to life before this cynic, and he was really
as incapable of action as Hamlet. Actually he
simply gave over the decision to the Jews.

History has long debated between the relative
guilt of Caiaphas and Pilate, and many have called
Caiaphas more guilty. But it is upon insufficient
grounds. Caiaphas knew the charge of treason
was groundless, but he *believed* in the charge of
blasphemy. Pilate believed in neither. He knew
both were unfounded. But he crucified the Lord
of Glory to keep his place in safety by playing to
the popular whim. And ringing down to the end

of the age goes his ignominious immortality, " Crucified under Pontius Pilate."

We have spent most of our time in analyzing
Pilate, and finding out what were the fatal flaws
in him which crucified Jesus Christ. Pilate had
the chance of his life, and he almost recognized it:
but he missed it because he did not trust his inner
light to recognize the Outer Light.

But have we not already seen our own timid,
ostentatious, sly, expedient selves standing there in
the Judgment Hall in the guise of Pilate, crucifying Christ with him? For are not the qualities in
Pilate which brought about the supreme tragedy
and shame of human history still found in us, mo-
tivating us while we crucify the Son of God afresh?

Which King do we really believe in the more—
Tiberius at Rome, with the world under his Roman
heel, and plenty of legions at his command—or
Jesus in His purple robe of mock-royalty, with a
handful of dejected Jews for His servants, and
twelve legions of imaginary angels nobody had
seen? Which do we believe in? Tiberius can get
things done. He can keep order hundreds of miles
away through men like Pilate. He can organize a
system of government to hold together the Roman
Peace. He can despatch Rome's best into the
provinces for the service of the State. Jesus' way
is very slow. He was unheard of even so near by
as in Rome. His Kingdom is invisible, a Kingdom
of peace in men's hearts, resting solely upon their
personal devotion to Him. It is a very precarious
Kingdom, dependent wholly upon what weak and

irresponsible men and women will do about it. And it is a very dangerous kingdom, for it has a way of leaping national and racial barriers and including all who love Jesus, and of assuming itself to be superior to every state organized by man, and to be man's absolute and first concern. Do we believe in the Force of Rome, more than in the Love of Christ? We've got to meet that honestly.

We, too, are torn every day of our lives between self-interest and wistfulness, between the expedient and the ideal, between the temporal and the eternal. Jesus is standing in the Judgment Hall of our own hearts this very morning, waiting for our sentence. He waits for it in your office, and in my study. He waits for it in what you will do for His little ones. He waits for it in the emphasis of your life. And it is so hard for us to decide what to do. We do not know which world is the realer—the outward or the inward: which world to work for, the temporal or the eternal. And while we stand there halting between the two, cynicism creeps upon us, skepticism, agnosticism: we are genuinely confused. We cry out, "What is truth!", and Jesus goes by default.

Oh my friends, your and my better and lower selves are incarnate in that Judgment Hall of long ago. Pilate stands for all the safety and compromise and utilitarianism and faith in the immediate and earth-crawling conservatism and man-made security which weight and hinder our lives. And Jesus stands for all the daring and courage and faith in the far-ideal and in the reality of the other world, which most bless and lift our lives. And the crucifixion to which Pilate put Jesus, after being once a historic fact, has become forever a recognized moral process, in which we all have part every time we sin. Jesus' was not such a kingdom that He could crucify Pilate. Pilate's was the guilt, but his was also the immediate power. Jesus' was the basic rightness, but His was also the immediate weakness. Which one are we crucifying in our own hearts to-day?

Jesus comes riding into Jerusalem this Palm Sunday, and the people welcome Him because they take Him for One Who will overthrow Rome and set up a Jewish state. But His " lowly pomp " as He enters into the city is the greatest sign of a worldly state that He shows. Day by day He teaches in the Temple, and night by night takes His way across Olivet. And before the week is out, the people are in a ferment because He means to overthrow, not Roman rule, but human sin, Jewish as well as Roman; and set up, not a Jewish state, but an everlasting Kingdom in the heart of universal man.

And coming up to Jerusalem the other way is Pilate. He lives in Cæsarea but he comes to Jerusalem for better order at the time of a great gathering like the Passover. He is not riding an ass, but probably a chariot: and he is surrounded by some of the three thousand soldiers who protect him. And he is obviously secure. And all who put their trust in him will also be secure. On the whole America believes in that kind of security:

it commends itself to us more easily than the invisible assurances of Jesus.

But you and I do not. We turn from Pilate and his kingdoms of this world as Jesus turned from the devil and his. The wistful in us is too strong.

And we are left asking ourselves the question which Pilate asked, " What then shall I do with Jesus which is called Christ? "

O God before Whom the long pageant of human life is passing, Thou with Whom are the real issues of our life: We do not always know whether we belong to the world or to Thee. Our faith is so feeble, and our trust in force is so strong. Press upon us this Holy Week the everlasting consequences of our daily choices. Show us where we crucify Christ again. And give us grace to die with Him, and so to come with Him to the joy of His resurrection. For His Name's sake. Amen.

VII

THE SEVEN LAST WORDS [1]

"Father, forgive them, for they know not what they do."
—St. Luke 23: 34.

FOR the next three hours, you and I are to fix our attention upon one scene. There is a Man on a Cross,—a cross made of common beams of wood, struck into the ground on top of a little hill, and lifting the Man but a very few feet above the others who stand about. The Cross was not very high, as it appears in some of the paintings. It was low enough so that Jesus' words, some of them perhaps hardly more than whispers, could be heard. Let us remember that in the glory of His agony He did not lift Himself magnificently above us: He was close to the little company of His friends and His enemies, so strangely mingled on that day. Let us note who stood near by.

There were four soldiers who stayed near Him, who had actually driven the nails and planted the tree, and who sat down to gamble for His one valuable garment: for the perquisites of the criminals belonged to their actual executioners. Jesus

* For much of the thought of these addresses, I gratefully acknowledge my debt to Dr. James Stalker's book *The Trial and Death of Jesus*, and I recommend it to the reader.

when He died, left a few pieces of common cloth-
ing and one woven coat without a seam—nothing
else, except His Gospel. Look well at this. God
in high heaven bending down to behold the utter-
most sacrifice of the One Perfect Life, the angels
watching " with sad and wondering eyes " to see
the atonement for all the sins of men forever—and
closest to the scene of all the sons of men, four
soldiers throwing dice for a piece of Jewish woven
cloth!

And then there were the members of the Jewish
Sanhedrin. The night before, these members of
the politico-religious court of the Jews had been
routed out very late, for a special meeting, called
by Caiaphas the High Priest to deal with Jesus
the Blasphemer Who made Himself equal with
God. It was illegal for them to sit at night, but
they made their decision and went home again, to
convene once more in the morning and make their
decision binding and lawful. This Man was a
menace to their traditional religion. They wanted
to be sure that He was put out of the way, and so
they followed the company of soldiers and morbid
hangers-on. And they moved about, a large company of them, throwing in His face the phrases
which He had used about Himself, " Son of God,"
" King of Israel," " Thou that destroyest the temple and buildest it in three days." And their
taunts, " Come down from the Cross, and we will
believe." Here were the defenders and protectors
of religion. And like wolves they devoured the one
indisputably perfect example of religion in history!

But, over to one side, there was a little group of His friends, those who had followed Him down from Galilee, taken in the tide of His happy mission up there by the side of the Sea of Gennesaret. Perhaps the larger proportion of them were women, and the record says that they stood " afar off." It was of no use to draw nearer, and they may have been prevented. The Master could see a little above the heads of those near Him. And here His eyes must have come to rest upon the frightened, distressed little company, who had forgotten His promise about resurrection, and saw in His present situation the blasting of all their hopes and the destruction of their faith. But at least they lingered with Him till the end.

Even though this scene is studied in all its historic detail, we yet cannot penetrate its meaning. We do not want to set our minds upon the physical details alone, ghastly and unforgettable as they are in their proof of Christ's love. We want to know what this all means—Perfect Love come to perfect cruelty at the hands of men, the Son of God the victim of politics and ecclesiasticism. How shall we know what it means?

There are seven words which Jesus spoke during those three black hours, and which are as windows into His own soul, revealing what He was thinking and feeling with all the intensity which suffering produces, with all the clarity that comes as we know the end is near, yet we are in full possession of our faculties. We shall take those words one by one and think about them, and let them stir thoughts and feelings and resolutions within us.

1

" Father, forgive them, for they know not what they do."

Let us break that up into its three parts and consider the salutation, the request, and the reason.

" Father," He begins. He spoke first to God. The first awful shock of pain was over, and His mind took its normal course again. It must have been a little relief to say His prayer aloud, and beside He wanted them standing by to hear. " Father." How that word must have rung through that company about the Cross! The believers were saying, " He still believes." The soldiers wondered what meant the mumbling of Aramaic words. And the priests and the Jews paused and said to themselves, " How can an impostor speak first to God in faith, if indeed he be an impostor! " Ah! many a heart was searched, and some were seared, by that first spoken word from the Cross, " Father." He knew whom He had believed, and was persuaded that He was able to keep that which He had committed unto Him even upon such a day.

" Forgive them." You must take your Bibles and study the four Gospel accounts of the betrayal and trial and crucifixion to understand what that includes. Remember the soldier who struck Him on the face, and the one who spat upon Him. Remember the priests twisting the law to their purposes; and Herod excited to see the Miracle-worker; and Pilate doubting his own purpose but too weak to stand for justice; and all the cruel, stupid mob that howled for His death and stayed together till they saw it accomplished. Picture the priests walking about the Cross in supreme satisfaction that they had got their way, and the poor dumb brutes of soldiers, with no wills nor minds of their own, as much victims of Rome's callousness alive, as Jesus was dead. And then look behind them to the systems which they represented and stood for. From out the welter of pagan and semi-pagan gods in whom the peoples of the eastern Mediterranean regions believed, the Jews had evolved faith in one God—one pure and Holy God, and they came to believe that He was not alone the God of the Hebrews but of all mankind. And in them faith and religion reached its zenith in the ancient world. One thinks of the long spiritual progress from Moses up to Isaiah and the prophets, dwelling upon Israel's moral duty toward their God. And then one sees all this slowly crystallized and frozen into forms of worship and stilted men without moral passion or spiritual insight, the mechanical mummies who preserved the shell of Jewish religion. And these soldiers represented Rome. The Mediterranean knew peace in those days, perhaps as much peace as any government could provide. But Rome had no altruistic motives. Beneath that peace went on constant strangulation of small, weak peoples, like the Jews. Jesus must have thought of all the indignity and injustice which they had done to His people. Few of us have ever had any real enemies, or ever had occasion for a great forgiveness. We know nothing of its cost or its meaning. But Jesus, seeing all this with transparent clarity, says only, " Forgive them." That was the first thing He asked of God.

And then He gave His reason, " for they know not what they do." Imagine His seeking for some excuse for the behaviour of His enemies in this hour, of all hours! Was it true that they knew not what they did? Judas knew. Pilate knew. Pilate's wife knew. Herod knew. The priests knew. They all knew that it was a piece of hurried injustice, in which they concurred because it was the easiest thing to do. But in the deeper sense they did not know. They did not know how much hung upon Jesus. They did not know that He would be the focal gathering-point for moral and spiritual values for all time. They did not know that in a vast, distant city, thousands of miles and thousands of years away, a thousand of us would be gathered here in a house called for that Hill of Calvary, to remember the death of Jesus, and them as parties to the great crime of history. But Jesus understood all that. He knew how unutterably guilty they were of what they did know but would not do; and for what they did in ignorance He prayed His Father's pardon.

Jesus always takes that attitude toward you and

me. We have hurt Him more times than we like to think. We have hurt Him by hurting His children: and we have hurt Him by being indifferent to Him. When His children suffer, Jesus is crucified. When His will is ignored, Jesus is crucified. But He looks above it somehow. And He prays to God for our forgiveness. The question for us to ask ourselves is, How much longer shall I take such love for granted?

2

" To-day shalt thou be with Me in Paradise."
(St. Luke 23: 43.)

We do not know by whose decision it was that Jesus was crucified between two malefactors, dying with Him in the same manner. Pilate might have ordered it. The Jews might have gained it as an additional shame to Jesus and identification of Him with the world's off-scouring. The soldiers may have done it themselves, with that rough sense of arrangement you sometimes find even in the brutalized, so that their most notable prisoner was framed between two lesser criminals. Long before, He had identified Himself with sinners and been called their friend. Now, by no will of His own, but surely with a consent which saw the divine meaning in it all, He was to die as one of them.

What, I wonder, should you and I have been feeling if we had found ourselves executed for our own misdeeds, but in the presence of Someone

Who did not seem to belong where He was in our company? In Jesus they found restraint and composure, while they writhed and screamed and cursed. He never lost His poise, " even in torture's grasp." And I suppose that it maddened them. He looked meek and wrongfuly handled, there was sadness in His face without bitterness. I fancy they hated Him because He would not come down to their level. And two of the Evangelists say that they both reviled Him along with the crowd. It identified them with the mob for a moment, and took the attention from them. Have you never joined in a good joke against a principle or a righteous person, when it made you solid with the majority of the company?

But as this went on, one of the men grew quieter. Jesus, I imagine, had refused to steel Himself in merely Stoical fashion against what was being said to Him and about Him. He heard what was said. And He neither flung out in hot rejoinder, nor retreated into Himself with eyes and mouth closed. He just somehow went on being loving. The thief may have travelled part of the way out from the city with Him, and heard that first prayer, and learned from the taunts of the crowd what were Jesus' claims. There is no evidence that he had ever seen Jesus before, or heard Him preach, or seen a miracle. What accounts for this so sudden change? We do not know. One has suggested that this may have been the renegade son of a religious home, and that something in Jesus reminded him of bygone days, and made him realize that the things he had heard at home were true after all. It is even possible that another mother stood below another cross, with an even more anguished heart than the Mother of Jesus: for her boy was dying, not for his faith but for his sins, he was unsaved, and perhaps she still prayed that he might repent.

If this be true, her prayer was most wonderfully answered in the last hours of her son's life. The accounts definitely say that both reviled Him. But one account says that one of the malefactors thus reviled Him, with the most natural taunt, " If Thou be the Christ, save Thyself and us." And the record in St. Luke goes on: " But the other answered, and rebuking him said, Dost thou not even fear God, seeing thou art in the same condemnation? And we indeed justly; for we receive the due reward of our deeds: but this man hath done nothing amiss. And he said, Jesus, remember me when Thou comest into Thy kingdom." And then, from Cross to cross, from Saviour to conscious penitent, went the wonderful message, " To-day shalt thou be with Me in Paradise."

The whole scene changed for that man. A few moments before he was the desperate criminal playing the desperado's part until the end, laughing with his companion at the powerlessness of Jesus Who made such great claims. Now he was a penitent, looking over into the face of his Saviour, seeing all his hopes centered in that dying Figure so triumphantly certain of God and eternal life. It is the supreme and classic instance of a sudden conversion. The Lord Jesus Christ raised no question about it, took the man's words as an index of budding faith, met it with His own promise of instantaneous companionship in the world beyond. Jesus certainly believed in its validity.

But what are we to say of sudden conversions now?

First we must remember that absolutely sudden conversions are rare: I mean those in which there is no preparation by spiritual exposure at some time in life. There are such: we have had a notable one in Calvary Mission, and it has been permanent. But there are few such; because there are few people who are not somewhere provided with the materials for later conversion, which are often stored in the cellars of the subconscious until some sufficient outer stimulus awakens memories, and the whole flares up into a complete right-about-face. St. Paul's experience was sudden, in that it took place instantaneously so far as eye could see. But upon his mind had been made one deathless imprint, and it was of Stephen dying. St. Augustine was converted as he read one verse in the New Testament, but he had a mother named Monica whom he knew all along to be praying for him. That is why childhood impressions and memories of religion, especially in our own homes, are of such incalculable and such indestructible worth: the child may grow up and wander far away from God, but he can never wander away from what his own memory cannot forget. It is

within the range of possibility that someone in this
church to-day should be broken down by bearing
for three hours the sight of Jesus' Cross, and give
his or her life completely to Christ, and go out a
different man or woman: I pray that it is so. And
that will be sudden if you like: but most of us
have indelible memories, gathered up like dry
fuel, waiting to be touched off into a blaze by some
agency from without. This may or may not have
been the case with the Penitent Thief—we simply
do not know, because we know nothing of his
background.

But the point is not by what inner process, slow
or rapid, the experience came. The point is that
he had within him spiritual insight to perceive at
his last hour that his whole life had been wrong,
and to see his true ideals and values incarnated
for him by the Man on the cross next to his, and
to admit this to himself, and then to say it aloud.
Possibly he said it in a moment when the crowd
had withdrawn, so that only a few could hear,
Jesus and someone who remembered and put it
into St. Luke's Gospel. But he said it. And it
makes us think of that great statement of St. Paul
that " with the heart man believeth unto righteousness; and with the mouth confession is made
unto salvation." And it turned his life for the few
hours left to him in this world, and for all the ages
of eternity.

There is only one possible danger in believing
in sudden conversion, and that is that we put off
the day of decision too long. For on the other

side of the Cross was another man, just like this one in all his outward life: they may have been companions in their crimes. But inwardly he was hopelessly different. All through the three hours till Jesus died, he went on feeling as he did at the first. Maybe he waked up after it was too late, and felt himself beyond all description desolate and forsaken and alone. Jesus' head had fallen and He could no more hear a word of petition. The thief across the hill had made his peace with Jesus and been promised eternal life that day. But he hung there in ghastly despair. I do not know if he tried to repent, or if he died hardened in his sins. In any case, the truth about him remains the same: he lost his chance to repent. Something in him would not break down, even in face of the holy living and dying that he saw next him.

Was ever such a picture of the flexibility and the obstinacy of human life as these two men on either side of the Cross! We can change if we will: and we can refuse to change if we will. In which class do we belong? When the Son of Man comes in His kingdom, no more the tortured plaything of priests and soldiers, but the King of Kings and Lord of Lords, He will still cleave men into these two groups; and one group will go away into outer darkness, and one will inherit the Kingdom with Himself. Where do we belong? It is a solemn thought. The thief had never seen Him before, and when he saw, he yielded. But we have seen Him many times. Have we any right

to expect Him to say to us, " To-day shalt thou be
with Me in Paradise," when we stand before Him
for judgment? Let us not trespass on His mercy.
But, like the thief, let us yield to His love.

3

*" Woman, behold thy son   .   .   .   Behold thy
mother."*
(St. John 19: 26–27.)

Even on the Cross, you will still find in Jesus
what you have found all along. He is God and
He is man. He will do some tremendous deed that
will make people want to kneel, and then He will
turn and do something kind and human and ten-
der that will make people feel something between
joy and tears. He has just promised Paradise to
a repentant thief. His next word is a word of human concern for His mother, not sent up to God,
but sent across the company to her and His fa-
vourite friend.

Simeon's prophecy had been made more than
thirty years before, that a sword should pierce
through her own soul also. She may have wondered through the years what he could have meant.
But now she knew: and as her memory swept in
anguish over the incidents in His life, from the
time when His little warm body lay in her arms
till this day when that same body hung torn and
bleeding upon the cross, this word must have come
back to her and brought the strange comfort that
our sufferings are foreseen by God and that some-

times we are made ready for them by the secret
which God has committed to one of His own.

And she stood as near the foot of the Cross as
she was allowed, unable to moisten the parched
lips or assuage the aching limbs which she would
have given her life to relieve. She was one of a
little company of three or four women, who had
followed Him and stayed with Him to the end.
There is a sad record that all His disciples forsook
Him and fled. But here were some of the women
who did not. There are places where women can
go and men cannot, places which men would make
more dreadful while women can sweeten them a
little. Not long since I heard from a very aged
and saintly woman of this parish how she got the
permission from President Lincoln personally to
go into the war area to see her husband who was
ill, and how she travelled with no other but a lone
coloured stewardess and hundreds of young re-
cruits, and how she went through all the hospitals
looking for her husband, not even noticing that
she had not eaten in two days. Men cannot do
without that sort of ministry of women: they become coarsened without it, and nothing else brings
so much restful peace. We may thank God de-
voutly that our Lord Jesus Christ had about Him
the comforting presence of women, and notably
of His own mother.

Whether St. John was included in that statement that " they all forsook Him and fled," we
cannot say. But if he fled, he soon realized his
mistake, turned about and came toward Calvary

with Jesus. He was the disciple whom Jesus loved. Jesus never favoured His intimates except by expecting of them greater fidelity: but He had His intimates, and the New Testament leaves no doubt that John was the first of them. " Peter, James and John " is the familiar group of the three apostles on whom He most heavily leaned—and it looks as though the greatest of these were John. Perhaps he entered more completely into his Master's plans, and understood His inner purposes. Perhaps it was one of those natural attachments which grow up out of the mystery of personality. It matters not—St. John alone of them all came with Him to the end, and we may take the liberty of imagining that Jesus would have wanted him above all the rest.

Jesus' relations with His mother are most interesting, and sometimes appear difficult to understand. He must at times have reverenced her with that love of one's mother which has often been observed to be almost a part of all fine humanity: but then there were times when He was the ageless Son of God and she was the temporal-minded Galilæan peasant. Once He turned upon her, if not savagely, at least with terrific finality, and said, " Woman, what have I to do with thee? Mine hour is not yet come." Never would He brook her interference with the broader plans of His life, as she and the rest of His family attempted to do once in Galilee. But this was in Him a means to keep pure His mission, and not, as it so often degenerates into being in us, thoughtless inattention to the rights of the family which is sometimes found in the public servant, be he philanthropist, preacher, reformer or missionary. I know of at least one such minister who made religion a hateful thing to his children because he would always rise from his table and fly to his study, as though his home were only a place for the satisfaction of his bodily wants. No, Jesus was not like this. Jesus, I imagine, carried His mother and the others of His family, with Him as far as they would or could enter into His hopes and His visions. He saw some things they did not see. He did not get caught up in so much detail and such fears as they. But He never left them out of His life and His heart. Now at the last He was thinking of provision for her.

It is most likely that St. John was unmarried, and there is some evidence that he may have been more comfortably situated than the other apostles. Jesus would not want His mother to be a burden. But I often think that Jesus would not have made this last request, asking so much as it did of them both—of the Virgin that she should virtually take John in His stead, and of St. John that he should take for a mother one who was not his mother— unless He had known that a great natural affection bound them together already. Most probably it was their common love for Him. Maybe all through the years they kept Him as the bond between them. There is a tradition that St. John never went outside of Jerusalem, even to preach the Gospel, but stayed there caring for the Mother

of his Lord so long as she lived: and only afterwards going to Ephesus with which we later asso-
ciate him. There is no reason known why she did
not go to one of her other sons. Perhaps Jesus
trusted St. John as He could not yet trust them.
The center of Mary's heart was the work which
Jesus had begun. With that John was more familiar and more in sympathy than any others. So
near were they in the fellowship of the Gospel that
there was no question of St. John's readiness to
accept the dying wish of his Friend. He commits
them one to the other.

There are two great lessons in this for us, which
endure for all time. And the first needs learning
by our age from the Master. Jesus' action was a
commentary,—and may have been a direct result
of His early teaching—upon the fifth command-
ment, " Honour thy father and thy mother, that
thy days may be long in the land which the Lord
thy God giveth thee." We are all concerned to-
day, who have eyes to see and minds to think,
with the breakdown of the home. There are vast
and intricate sociological reasons given for it, and
equally vast and complicated sociological cures
recommended. But in the last analysis it comes
back to us as individuals. How do we feel about our
family? Are they sources of revenue, or sources of
irritation, or sources of deep fellowship? The way
to prevent broken homes plainly is to develop with
our own parents real relationships, to take the
time and trouble needful for that, to learn how to
enjoy them, and to share with them our real in-

terests. Such homes do not break up with the
children scattered from dawn till all hours of the
night. Let us think of the Holy Family as something besides a beautiful canvas in a museum: let
us think of it as composed of independent units
like our homes, but through these let there be
woven the golden thread of the life of the Eldest
Brother. Let Him still be the shining, golden
thread.

And the next lesson is that Jesus is concerned
about human necessaries, " as well for the body as
the soul." Wherever His Gospel has gone, there
has gone also mercy toward the homeless, the
aged, the sick and the destitute. In His Name
countless thousands of hospitals, asylums, homes,
shelters have been built. In some cases these have
become so secularized that His Name is a name
only and no longer a force: and it is an infinite
pity that it is so. But where they are true to their
first impulse, these merciful ameliorations go on
showing how much Jesus has done to save our
world. And they have His word for their charter,
" Inasmuch as ye have done it unto one of the
least of these My brethren, ye have done it unto
Me." It was not so before He came. It is not so
where His word has not gone out to the ends of
the earth. Something of the flavour of kindness
as it was in Jesus has come down into His Church
and His followers—not enough of it, not broad
enough, not deep enough, not good enough, but
still it is there. And all who think at all realize
what it means to the world. Some time when you

are asked to give for these places, and your heart
grudges a little, remember this picture of Jesus on
His Cross. In His Mother He beheld all lonely,
pitiful, defenseless folk forever. He took thought
for her. He expects us in His Name to take
thought for them.

4

*"My God, My God, why hast Thou
forsaken Me?"*
(St. Mark 15: 34.)

I suppose that this is the most awful word that
ever rang across the air of this world. It is
scarcely a wonder that from the sixth hour till the
ninth—these three hours beginning at noon which
we are now keeping—there was darkness over all
the land, as though the sun veiled his face, as
though nature drew the curtains round this black-
est sin of man. Out of the cloudy darkness comes
this cry that is darker than any cloud. I used
to think that this marked the one failure of Jesus,
the collapse of His faith. I used to hate to read
these words: I wanted to pass them by, and forget
that He ever gave way to them. But that was a
shallow fear and lack of understanding. Now I
thank God that He said them, and I pray that
you may do so also before you leave this church
to-day.

We are all confronted with an inexplicable life,
and sometimes with a very bitter life. We see
sorrow come, like the rain, upon the just and upon

the unjust. We wonder at the meaning of evil in the world when we believe in a good God. We take a general interest in all this when it comes near us, in our friends or neighbours: but then there comes a day when suffering falls right down upon us, and it is all drawn down out of the general and the academic into the immediate and personal. And here what we really are comes out. We tend to react in two directions. We crumple up and go to pieces, our nerves give out, self-pity seizes us, and we go under—or we stiffen ourselves, fight down our nerves, turn Stoic, and glaze the surface of our minds till we make the suffering run off like water from a smooth wall. It is the experience of our life that neither of these is a satisfactory solution to the problem of human trouble. And I ask you to notice that Jesus took trouble in a wholly different way.

He was neither crushed by it, nor did He make Himself indifferent to it. He let it fall full-force upon Him first, so that He might have the full experience of it, and so both understand all that we suffer, and also draw out from it all that it was intended He should learn by it. That is why you hear Jesus say so often just exactly what He felt, not shutting it up within Himself nor keeping it from those about Him whose faith He might have feared to shake. At the beginning of this Holy Week some Greeks were brought to Him by two of His disciples: and one imagines that He saw in these spiritual seekers an epitome of the great pagan world outside. It might have stirred Him to great joy that they sought Him: but instead it caused Him acute sadness, for He knew that He would not live long enough to carry on His campaign in their territory. And He spoke out, " Now is My soul troubled, and what shall I say? Father, save Me from this hour: but for this cause came I unto this hour." It was a profound expression of human bafflement and frustration, connected with His clear vision of the coming Cross: and He said it out where His friends could hear it. And again this all comes out most clearly in Gethsemane. He took the three intimates with Him, and in the Garden He fought out in terms which it is not difficult for us to understand, the final unification of His own will with the will of God for the redemption of the world. He flinched from the Cross as we should, flinched at the pain, flinched at the shame, flinched at the sign of failure, flinched at the interruption of His work, flinched with wonder how it could be that, having lived always in the spirit of love, He must die as though He had done wrong. He did not throw all this off lightly: He let it all trouble His mind and disturb His heart. The human Jesus suffered as a human Man, till the sweat rolled off Him like drops of blood. Three times did His will register its decision, only slowly bringing the willingness of His emotions into line, " Nevertheless, not My will, but Thy will be done." Now there happened at that moment, upon a stupendous scale of progressive self-dedication, the same thing which happens for us when we surrender, though for us

it always means a break with our past while for
Him it meant a fulfilment of His own life of perfect obedience. We can follow Him here—we
often must, and some of us do. And we know that
when we surrender with our whole wills, something
happens that never wholly disappears. New
ground is taken which we never entirely lose.

But we know, too, that such a decision of the
will does not insure that we shall always be able
to keep our emotions in line with it. Sometimes
they will break away from that decision within a
short time. Now I am moving from the human
to the divine, from what we can fully understand
in ourselves to what we cannot fully understand
in Christ: but I feel sure that it was *something*
like this which happened on the Cross, and made
Him cry out, " My God, My God, why hast Thou
forsaken Me? " There was, we may feel sure, a
physical element in that cry. The time wore on.
The pain grew worse. If He tried to shift His
body and give it any easement from its torture,
the pain was only made more intolerable. And we
cannot but believe that the pain was worse for
Him, not only because of a sensitive organization
which was the human habitation of His sensitive
spirit; but because death was coming on, and
there was no real connection between Him and
death. Death came by sin, and He knew no sin.
But these are not the deepest things that lie behind that cry.

Last night in Gethsemane He had struggled to
keep His *will* poised toward the will of God, and

He had succeeded. Now there is a new struggle
in His *mind*. " Why " is the philosopher's question. It is the first expression of a troubled mind.
It may come out of the vacant detachment of a
mind that never really lives in the world, and asks
coldly and objectively. But here it rose from a
tortured mind. The utmost of human physical
suffering was upon Him. He felt literally the sins
of the whole world weighing upon His spirit. It
seemed as if He could not bear it. There are
times in our experience when everything seems to
go wrong, there can no longer be plan or reason in
anything: and we look up to God out of our desolation and say, Why? That cry may be one of
petulance and self-pity; it often is: or it may arise
out of a just and delicate mind, jealous for the
love and justice of God to be proved. Belief in
God's care is necessary to it. It cannot bear the
thought that God is unfair or unconcerned. All
this fell upon Jesus without deference to His goodness or divinity. He took upon Him our nature,
and He endured all the possible experiences of that
nature except sin. Do you know what I believe
this is? I believe that it is the place in Jesus' life
where He, without sinning, knew what it feels like
to be a sinner: for the sharpest of all the pains of
sin is the banishment from God. Sin does not
actually banish God by making God turn away
from us; God comes hovering over us more than
ever. But the effect upon us is the same: sin itself builds the wall that hides God out. You have
felt that, and so have I, and never at any other

time was life so utterly destitute as then. This did not come upon Jesus by sin, but it came upon Him in His unique character of sin-bearer. Yes, I believe that here Jesus knew all the desolation which we know through our sins, magnified, intensified, infinitely, agonizingly worse because the whole experience for Him was unjustified and vicarious. It was the place in His life where, for a brief and bitter season, He touched the awful utmost of human forsakenness. Even God seemed gone. Does that disturb your faith in Jesus Christ? It vastly deepens mine. If I felt that there were agonies of human suffering from which He was exempt, if I had known in my own soul depths of desolation to which He was alien, He never really could be my Saviour. I might look up to Him for a fine dream, but I should know in my mind that He was beyond me, hopelessly and forever beyond me. There would be some things in my life which He had not undergone. But if here He felt with me the utter solitude and despair of sin, borne vicariously but borne really, then He can be my Saviour. None who experienced the sin itself could be—he would be in my class. *Jesus is in my straits without being in my class.* Get that, my friend, and carry it home with you and believe in it forever. Here is where your Lord touched bottom for you. Let it bring Him close to you till you know that He understands you and carries with you your life.

And remember, too, that none who can still say " My God " is wholly forsaken. There was faith

down in the heart of His cry of despair, as often
there is in ours. There is prayer here as well as
question. The prayer was answered. It was a
mood, and the mood passed. We shall hear Him
speak again presently in His usual calmness of
spirit.

5

" I thirst."
(St. John 19: 28.)

Our last meditation was upon the darkest moment in human history. Out of Jesus' cry of forsakenness came victory. That this had happened
seems to be confirmed by the way in which St.
John introduces this fifth word, " After this, Jesus,
knowing that all things were now accomplished,
that the Scripture might be fulfilled, saith, I
thirst." The phrase " that the Scripture might be
fulfilled " refers back to the " knowing that all
things were now accomplished," for there is no
prediction in the Old Testament that the Messiah
should say, " I thirst."

He had been offered something to drink at the
moment when they reached Calvary. " The
wealthy women of Jerusalem had a practise of
providing a soporific draught for those condemned
to the awful punishment of crucifixion. It was
composed of wine mixed with some narcotic drug
like gall or myrrh, to dull the senses and deaden
the pain." This was given to all criminals, no
matter what their crime, and the authorities per-

mitted them this amelioration of their pains. Jesus had gone through an agonized and sleepless night, and had tried to drag His cross upon His own back toward Calvary. He must have been bitterly thirsty, weary and conscious of the terrible ordeal of pain that awaited Him. He took up the draught, put it to His lips, and then put it down again. He would not drink. He would meet death in the full possession of His faculties, and in the full feeling-capacity of His senses. Thank God for the merciful office of morphia and ether in eliminating needless human pain: but there comes a pain from which we dare not run away, at the risk of our own souls. Jesus was not a fanatic about such things, as we see by the word we are considering: but neither would He be a slave to them.

Why then did He finally ask for something to drink? One has suggested that as He refused the first draught in order to keep His mind clear, He accepted the second for the same reason. He would make these things minister in every case, not to bodily satisfaction, but to spiritual ends. And that is still the distinction which differentiates the use of drugs in the right way from their use in the wrong way: what does it do to human character?

This is Jesus' one cry of physical necessity from the Cross. It was not a cry of pain or of rebellion, it was a request for help. I ask you not to forget that in all the other words of Jesus there is not a suggestion about His own needs and pain, but only a high concern about other people and about the spiritual significance of what has been happening to Himself. Here is surely a courage and a patience which we must stop to notice. There is no record that Jesus was ever sick. I suppose, therefore, that He was a man of good health, who knew weariness and hunger, but not pain and suffering. Oftentimes the long-time sufferers come to terms with their pain, have a kind of understanding with it; Sir James Barrie says that his mother, Margaret Ogilvy " bore physical pain as if it were a comrade." But pain is a different problem for healthy people. It is we who are most put out by it, make most of its least exactions, and become an exasperation to our households and a trial to our doctors, just because we make so much of so little. Let us recall, next time we fancy that we are much afflicted with pain, the silent suffering of our Lord, which never asked to be ministered to in more than what would correspond, for us, with a glass of water. " I thirst." What a request to make of a world to which He had given its richest treasure!

Just where you think that Jesus is utterly beyond you in divine power and self-control, He opens a window that you may look in upon His full humanity. Perhaps we here in this church have already begun to take in something of the magnitude of what is happening on Calvary, and we may almost feel the Christ receding, going beyond us in His incomprehensible courage and beauty of spirit. Let this little word remind you

how completely He is one with us in flesh and
blood, " I thirst." There never was foolish as-
ceticism in Him, unrelated to His work, as sometimes there has been in His followers, like Simeon
Stylites up his pillar, a spiritual clown for men to
watch, instead of a spiritual servant to serve them;
and many a cloistered man and woman that had
better have had on overalls than a cowl, and an
apron than a habit. All Jesus' self-denial—and
there was much of it—aimed ultimately at His
spiritual service. He gave up one that He might
do the other better. There was ever about Him
the sweet reasonableness of common sense. And
He kept close to the great body of people, as far
as possible from being a spiritual eccentric. " I
thirst." Nothing else that He said on the Cross
could have come from us; but you and I, in His
place on a cross, might have said that.

I want you to see a contrast here. This was an
exposure of His own need which stood up ill beside some of His claims. It was not so long since
He had stood in the Temple and cried, " If any
man thirst, let him come unto Me and drink. He
that believeth on Me, as the Scripture hath said,
from within him shall flow rivers of living water."
And now this Great Promiser hung on a Cross,
with His own body parched and bleeding, calling
for someone to bring Him something to drink!
You remember Him travelling up toward Galilee
from Judæa, and stopping by a well-side, and talking to a Samaritan woman and saying " Whoso-
ever shall drink of this water shall thirst again:

but he that drinketh of the water that I shall give him shall never thirst; but the water that I shall give him shall be in him a well of water springing up into everlasting life." And now the position was all reversed, He was not the Promiser but the Asker. He was not in the bountiful position, but in the position of suppliant. There is a manifest thread of unity in Jesus' life, by which He was always magnificently and unbrokenly Himself. But He never looked for a consistency to which He might appeal. He trusted us to see that there was a difference between inward wealth and outward poverty, between having the riches of the ages to confer in matters of the spirit, and often not having a place to lay His head. Think now of the humility of the Son of God, asking the group of His enemies for something to cool His tongue! Did it sound like defeat? No mind—He asked for it. Did it look like capitulation to His enemies? They were not enemies to Him: He had commended them to God's forgiveness. It was, from the human side, the most exposing word He said on the Cross; it looked most like physical, human weakness. But He did it. Jesus never feared to be Himself, to show His heart when it might come back upon Himself in misunderstanding. But sometimes He froze into silence when men asked Him what spiritual motives prompted Him, when they had no right to ask or to know.

But I want you to take a broader view of this fifth word. It is a glimpse into the desire of Jesus. It lets us see for a moment, in the days of His flesh, a tiny, physical thing which He desperately wanted, with the burning thirst of those dying of pain. All that is gone by forever. The wood of the Cross is long since rotted and gone back again into the earth from which it grew. But still, in the great heart of the Everlasting Christ, a thirst burns. He longs for something with a longing unspeakable. Even in high heaven, He is not satisfied. He still suffers from a burning thirst. It is a thirst to see this world one believing family, brothers toward each other, and children toward God. Every tiny cup with a drink of brotherhood in it, He blesses. Every draught with a taste of faith in it, He hallows. Every effort to clear the minds of men of prejudice, to wash the wills of men of unbrotherliness, to lift the feelings of men to generosity, bears a cup to His eternal lips, and slakes the everlasting thirst of God. I ask you to see in this that He thirsts for you, for your character and righteousness, for your joy and happiness, for your faith and blessedness. We love to think that if we had caught His cry from the Cross, we should have started this way and that, and *somewhere* found Him a drink to quench His thirst. Remember the Cross always at the heart of God, the Lamb slain from the foundation of the world. Look up and see through the skies the parched lips of Christ in heaven. Lift up the only cup you have, the cup of your life, the cup of your love. Hold it to His lips. Press Him to drink of it and be satisfied. Tell Him you were not there to quench His thirst on Golgotha, but you will quench it now if He will accept your offering. That is all that satisfies Christ. All His thirst is toward the lives of men and women and children. Nothing is such joy as to drink when you are thirsty. Let Christ drink the devotion of your life.

6

" It is finished."
(St. John 19: 30.)

No man ever undertook the work which Jesus undertook. I ask you to think for a little of the gathering purpose of that one life, the rush and force of that single torrent down its narrow channel, and the amazing power which carried down the stream with it so much that had been cluttering the whole river-bed of human existence, making its course sluggish and turgid. When He was a lad of twelve He felt that purpose, and the only sight we see of Him, from His babyhood at Bethlehem and Nazareth until His " shewing unto Israel," is His surprised question of His parents, " Wist ye not that I must be about My Father's business? " And later in the full plenitude of His powers He says, " I have a baptism to be baptized with, and how am I straitened till it be accomplished! " And again, " I have meat to eat that ye know not of. My meat is to do the will of Him that sent Me, and to finish His work." It was not a frenzied, fanatical passion that wore out His nerves, and made Him irritable with those who would not share it; but it was none the less a pure, high, tense, constant, unrelenting passion. He awoke with prayer about it in the morning, and He laboured quietly about it all day and He used even His resting hours apart to make ready for His great purpose. You will often see Him stop by a roadside, or call little children to Him, or seek a desert place apart: He has the leisure of the saunterer, but not his aimlessness. It was leisure through a peaceful and unified spirit; it was never the leisure of them without purpose. Often in these casual conversations His best work was done, and His finest disciples recruited. In His heart burned the undying fire which warmed and lighted His life.

What was it? He came into a world outwardly and politically more quiet than it had been for a long time. That stiff, dead peace called the Roman peace, kept things in their places about the Mediterranean. Governments are always eager to manifest the signs of peace in the subject countries which they annex. But beneath all this unnatural stillness there seethed the unquenchable love for freedom in the human heart. It was an awful temptation to Him to become a political liberator. That was what the people longed for. Be sure that a Man who could say, " Follow Me," and have them follow, could also manage soldiers and politicians. Jesus knew the heart of man, and do not fear that He could not have made Himself a political force, even without lowering His standards, if He had chosen to. We have seen through the activity of Mahatma Gandhi that the prophet still has power in the practical world, a curious power which the governments half despise and half fear. Jesus weighed all that in His great temptation, and put it behind Him forever. He would win liberty for men, but a deeper liberty than any throwing-off of a Roman yoke. He would free them from themselves. I believe that we are wrong to think that all the while He was asking Himself how He could interpret God to men, as though He had been sent into the world to work only for God. I am sure that He grew up with normal patriotism and humanity, asking Himself also how He could interpret man to himself, and how God might help man with his problems. From the one side, I am sure that He was the Revealer of God and His special Ambassador: but from the other, I am sure that He was also a thoroughly representative and socially-minded Man, interested in the things which concerned His own nation, and all mankind, and eager to bring religion specifically to bear upon these things.

So that we may say that His work was two-fold. He had to make men know what God is, and He had to help them to see that God was the solution to their problems. It was therefore a life of teaching, of faith-making and of persuasion. He invested Himself in the invisible forces of standards and values and inner attitudes. He believed ultimately in personality as against institutions, in faith as against rules for conduct, in persuasion as against force. He took the most tenuous and frail-appearing factors in our life, and treated them as if they were immense coils of rope, bulwarks of stone, and armies of soldiers. " Your faith hath saved you," He would cry. " Except ye become as little children, ye cannot enter My Kingdom." " My Kingdom is not of this world." " Resist not evil, but overcome evil with good." These things were foolishness to the sophisticated, the worldly-wise, the humourless cynics and Philistines who constitutionally could not understand Him: but they were the power of God and the wisdom of God to those who believed.

But, dear me, how could anybody say that there was anything " finished " about that process? It isn't within the remotest range of being finished now. Men generally do not believe in those ulti-mate forces any more than they did when He was here. The law of politics is not much different from the law of the jungle. Thousands of men are utterly indifferent to God and have no idea that He matters a farthing in human life. How can anybody say that Jesus' work was finished?

Now there is something daring and a little breath-taking about this statement of His. It looks like an over-statement. But I do not believe that it is.

For, in the first place, Jesus' own life was com-plete. It is not fullness of years, or mere quanti-tative achievement which marks a complete life. It is a quality of perfectness in the life itself. Many have done more and lived more whose lives were never complete. Completeness is really a matter of inner wealth and peace. It is a quality

of self-sufficiency in the presence of the bafflements
and perplexities and sufferings of life, or rather a
matter of God-sufficiency. In that sense, so far
as His own character was concerned, our Lord's
life could have been cut off anywhere and still it
would have been " finished " in the sense that He
had, by His obedience, won His own soul and
earned the everlasting worship of all the sons of
men by being and remaining what He was.

But His life was complete in a richer sense also.
True, He was in His early thirties, and that He
only left behind Him a handful of followers for
all His pains. True, He died on a hilltop surrounded by His enemies, forsaken by most of His
friends. True, the world called Him a failure, and
still calls defeat and shame gained in causes of
human redemption by the same name to-day.
Nevertheless, it was an amazing success—amazing
as only He, with eyes of pure and selfless insight
could see. I think that the thing which made Him
say " It is finished " was the knowledge that He
had lived long enough to infect the world with a
new principle. What He saw about Him were the
ashes of a dead world—militarism, irreligious
priestcraft, broken, hunted human lives, punishment without redemption toward the thieves,
blind, purposeless cruelty and bitter, inexplicable
suffering. Crosses stopped with the Cross, and
most of the world's evils began to stop there also.
The Cross hauled the world up before its own bar,
and said, " You are living by the wrong principles,
for the wrong ends. You do not know where you

really want to go, and to go on the way you are
travelling at present means disaster." The world
is still shocked by that thought—*maybe we are all
wrong!* We have never gotten over the blow of
Christ's victory in defeat. It has turned all our
tables upside down, and tilted our values. When
we are brutes to each other, when we gouge and
kill and hate each other, there is an awful feeling
in our hearts that this is not what life was meant
to be, that it is not what life *needs* to be. Jesus
has at least planted an almost universal misgiving
in the mind of the world, that worldliness is the
way out. Paganism never doubted that. What
other world was there to think about? Men were
reduced to their own thoughts and their own cures.
But Jesus opened a "new and better way." The
world had always believed that victorious force
was the ultimate thing to seek and was the final
sign of success: Jesus showed us for all time that
the most powerful thing in all this world is suffering love, and that what may be signed with the
Cross may alone be called successful. Very few
believe that enough to dare to live by it: but that
was new with Jesus. And amid all the dangers
of its loss these two thousand variegated years, we
have not lost the thought of it. Jesus looked down
into the very few faithful faces about Him, and
remembered the few others who would come back
and be loyal again: and He must have said to Himself, " This little handful, the whole fruit of My
labours, is the one hopeful society in the world,
the only true ' initiates ' in the open secret of how

to live, the vanguard of the new humanity. They got what I said. They saw the point. They dared to follow. They will carry on. It is finished! "

We are their spiritual descendants. Can He look down from His Cross into our faces, and then lift His own heart to God, having seen the travail of His own soul, and been satisfied?

7

" Father, into Thy hands I commend My Spirit."
(St. Luke 23: 46.)

The words on the Cross began with a prayer, and they ended with one. Prayer was the spirit of the Cross, and even the words He said to men —to the thief, to His mother and His friend, and to the soldiers—were bathed in prayer. In the hidden traffic of His soul with God He had found the meaning of His life. When death approaches, it is with confidence and with relief that He says, " Into Thy hands I commend My Spirit." These words are also a quotation from Scripture. And I want you to see in Jesus now, not the Revolutionary, but the Rememberer; not the Man Who founded a new religion, but the Man Who had His roots deep in the past of an old religion. The hour of death may be said to be too late an hour to be original: when we are dying, provided we are ourselves at all, we are ourselves entirely. The habits of a lifetime come out. We say and do what is characteristic of us; it grows up out of the fields where our minds and hearts have been feeding all the years. In a sense, Jesus did for Himself what His people still do for themselves, or ask one of their family, or one of His ministers to do for them, He prayed and He quoted the Scriptures. A wholly godless death is often a terror to behold, and a deeply Christian death is a blessing which to behold may free the mind forever from the fear of one's own last hours. Jesus almost passed over the thought of the article of physical death, and in His Spirit leaped out and up toward the mansions of light, toward His Home.

There was here no mere hope of everlasting life. This prayer assumed everlasting life. Jesus expected to have given to Him again the life He now gave to God, the life rent from its physical house by death. The most solemn question any of us can ever ask is, " If a man die, shall he live again? " With one part of our nature, we seem condemned to the same nothingness as the trees which rot and the animals which disappear. But with another part, we seem to require a spiritual existence in which our spirits have free rein and true deliverance. No age is free of those who play upon the difficulty of believing in immortality and our age is riddled with those who believe nothing so much as that we are only animals after all. I say, on the other side, that there are simply those in this world who do not live like animals and do not die like them, and I do not expect to see them treated like animals in the final disposition. If you can say to me with confidence that you think Jesus' life stopped when His body died on Golgotha, I must ask you to explain to me the reunited disciples, the sudden increase in the Christian Church, the conversion of Saul of Tarsus, and the host of men and women to-day who ascribe the deepest joy in their lives to their relation to a risen, living, glorified Christ. But when all is said and done, we all believe in immortality principally because our Lord believed in it Himself, had no question when He inclined His head and died as we shall all die, that He would awaken in the presence of His Father, and gave us a most glorious promise in the words, " Because I live, ye shall live also." But this last act of Jesus on the Cross is only what we should have expected of Him. It is the natural ending of a life spent in doing God's will. He said it without fear, with perfect naturalness and with perfect faith. The days of His flesh were over. Henceforth His Kingdom was to be a spiritual Kingdom where He ruled the hearts and consciences of men by the influence of His human life, and by His living Spirit in the world.

And now let us take one final look at the Cross, and try, if we may, to sum up what it all means.

It certainly means that somewhere, on a gigantic scale, a catastrophe has taken place in our universe. This is the most tremendous reversal of ordinary human judgments in history: it is like a vast stick in the stream of common human life attempting to change its course. It is surely a mighty wrestling with a mighty problem. That God's Son should deliberately and willingly be ranged and ranked with criminals in order to say something, through the very spectacular paradox of it, to humanity, is enough to take our breath and make us look into our whole view of life. Mankind has had the insight to rescue from the oblivion of time this apparently trivial incident of One Man's execution for seemingly seditious and blasphemous ideas, and to see in it the most stupendous of moral significances, and the greatest of all spiritual meanings. We have seen in it God Himself, taking upon Himself the enormity of man's sin, and bearing it in our stead.

Let us forget now the nails and the thorns and all the physical part of it. Let us for a moment try to see things as God sees them. Let us remind ourselves of the holiness and of the love of God. With infinite love does He love the sons of men, and He wants that love to be the only compulsion they have to be good and to believe. Man, on the other hand, has grown hideously indifferent to that love and the law which attaches to all love: in superb independence he tries to make his way without God, and by it he falls into sin. Not only is the love of God repudiated, but the holiness of God is outraged. Love divine is not blind: God sees us as we really and essentially are. We are offenders against His law, as well as rejectors of His love. Love may not say much about being outraged, and the restraint of the Cross in its condemnation of man is one of the most amazing things about it: but God sees facts for facts. And the fact is that sin is always a personal affront to

God. It is setting up a law of our own in defiance of His. What shall God do? Shall He close the door on man forever? Man deserves nothing better: if God had left us alone forever it would have been merited by our indifference to God. Or shall God weakly condone man's sin, and make wrong to appear right? There is no ultimate hope in that kind of dishonesty. What then shall God do? We dare not answer that question, save to try to interpret what He did do. What He did was to get under man's sin Himself, absorb the weight and shock of it, let its blow fall upon Him instead of us, enter fully into our situation and carry our sin with us. Something of this is surely the meaning of the statement, " He made Him to be sin for us Who knew no sin, that we might be made the righteousness of God in Him."

You say to me, How can one person " bear " the sins of another? Let me tell you a story. Some weeks ago a friend of mine who is a minister of Christ had a man come to him in desperate spiritual need. Like most of those who are in great spiritual need, he was also in great temporal and financial need as well. The minister asked him to stay at his house. But the man's pride was too great for that, he said—he had at least always made his own way. Now the chief thing that was the matter with that man was not the sin of his body, but the sin of his mind; not his lust and his drunkenness, but his pride. Before he could be rid of his gross sins, something must break down his pride. There was no way to break it down except to make him *accept something he didn't deserve, to give him something which it was literally impossible for him to pay for*. He finally consented to come: and with his pride down, he was in position to accept something else than hospitality from the minister, and he found Christ through him. The minister paid both the board-bill and the cost of giving that man hours of time to redeem him. The man gave nothing and received twice: the minister got nothing and gave twice. But the process of redemption began at the moment when the man *accepted something which he knew he did not deserve, and was given something which it was literally impossible for him to pay for*. That is what I call " bearing " another person's sins. And that is the precise and definite aim of the Cross of Christ: to destroy our pride by persuading us to accept a gift which we do not deserve, by giving us something which we could not possibly pay for. There is no more subtle or dangerous pride in the world than the pride of being righteous without God's help. The indispensability of the Cross lies here: that the man whose righteousness comes up out of himself is bound to be self-righteous,—and self-righteousness is worse than no righteousness at all. We can only be really good by derivation. We can only really be good by being given something to be thankful for. The man, therefore, who knows beyond doubt that he has been saved through the atoning death of Jesus Christ has no place left in his life for pride—all he has is abashed and astonished thankfulness. The Cross is a frontal attack of God upon man's pride. Its first and chief message is, " You cannot save yourself! "   Salvation comes through the mercy of God, not through the merit of man.

But the Cross does something else beside crushing the pride out of us. It restores us as the conscious children of God's love. Its final word is not concerned with how little we *can do* for ourselves, but with how much God *has done* for us. It ought to make us think of the cost of our salvation to God: but the heart of it is, " Never mind the price—it has been paid."

St. John looked up one day to see Jesus, and said, " Behold the Lamb of God, which taketh away the sin of the world." On the Cross of Calvary the Lamb died a sacrifice for us. Has He taken away the sins of the world?   Your life and mine are the answers to that: our response to the Cross is the only measure of it.   He certainly gave to us, to as many as would receive it, the holiest motive that ever stirred a human heart—the desire not to wound further the suffering love of God.   And He certainly provided in the Cross a fountain of everlasting grace to help in time of need.   Thousands upon thousands down the Christian centuries have looked up to the Cross and said that from the moment they accepted it as their pledge of salvation, their lives began to mend. That may begin for you, my friend, to-day.   Let us take heed lest we " neglect so great a salvation."

I close with a quotation from the mystic Jacob Böehme:

"The suffering and death of Christ avail only for those who die to their own will in and with Christ, and are buried with Him to a new will and obedience and hate sin; who put on Christ in His suffering, reproach and persecution, take His Cross upon them and follow under His red banner; to those who put on Christ in His process and now become in the inward spiritual man Christ's members and the Temple of God who dwells in us. No one has a right to comfort himself with Christ's merits unless he desires wholly to put on Christ in himself. He is not a Christian until he has put Him on by true repentance and conversion to Him with absolute resignation and self-denial, so that Christ espouseth and betrotheth Himself with him. . . . For a Christian must be born of Christ and must die to the will of Adam. He must have Christ in him and be a member of His Life according to the spiritual man."

VIII

POST-CRUCIFIXION CHRISTIANITY

"Did not our heart burn within us, while He talked with us by the way?"—St. Luke 24: 32.

I HAVE never understood how anyone could feel that there is any antagonism between evolution and revelation in religion. You will now and then find people who say that Christianity was dropped straight out of heaven at one time, complete in all its moral principles and all its theological truth; and that to add to, or subtract from, that perfectly finished system is to be false to Christianity. The difficulty with that kind of a theory is the question where and when this all happened. You say, " It happened in Christ Himself." Yes, but Christ lived and worked above thirty years: and even that was not the end of His activity. There was an evolution in the revelation of Christ, as men progressively found out more about His meaning, and discovered Him to be potent in situations where they had not imagined Him before.

There are three very marked stages in that development, which are made plain by the great crisis of the Crucifixion. The first stage is that before the Crucifixion. When Jesus first walked beside the Sea of Galilee, He was a wandering teacher, a Prophet, the Beginner of a movement for the purification of the lives of the people and the Pleader for a fresh experience of God. Men and women were drawn to Him because of the things He said, the wonderful stories He told, stories which grew up out of their common life, and yet had significance as far as their imaginations could see. He was the Revealer of simple moral truth. He talked about the elementary human obligations and relationships; He made the friendship of God seem a glorious reality. In those early days He did not say very much about Himself: He said a good deal about God, and a good deal about high and fine living. I suppose that people joined Him because He seemed to be so incontestably right in the things He said about life, and because there was something irresistible about Him personally. The most acute and critical note in these days was the question whether a man would give up everything to follow Him. There was as yet no great intellectual problem to solve. The question of His Person they were too immature to ask or to understand. They were mostly practical-minded Jews, not over-troubled about such problems as evil and pain: the way to solve those questions was the way Jesus was solving them, to do away with them so far as there was power on the one side, and faith on the other, which made possible the doing away with them. This first picture of Christ is a happy picture, and the severity of His moral demands is softened by the tremendous beauty of His own life.

But across this happy picture the clouds began to gather as the days went on. He was at liberty, legally and spiritually, to say pretty much what He chose out through the country districts. He could gather in whom He would, and make followers of them. But two things began to emerge. The first was that Jesus thought Himself to be something more than a Teacher; and it only took time until the rest saw it, and Simon Peter's great confession of faith in His divinity must have been really spoken for them all. And this was at variance with orthodox Judaism, and sooner or later was likely to clash with it. So that the second thing which emerged was the slowly unfolding antagonism which Jesus felt for the Jewish religious system; an antagonism which was fully returned on their side. Hostility grew out of this widening breach, until the outward facts corresponded with the inward conviction of Jesus that He must die. This was a very far cry from the lilies of the field and the gentle days of Galilee. Simon rebuked Him for thinking about it. Apparently it never quite entered their minds that He meant what He said when He told them that He must die. But He knew very well that it would turn out as it did: and in this great second period of Christianity, the Cross has begun to cast a shadow backward across the company of disciples, forcing them to reckon with something dark and sinister which they had not reckoned with before. They went on to Jerusalem, and just as He told them it would, it all came out; the Sanhedrin took Him and made away with Him. Of course the sharpest climax of this Crucifixion period of Christianity was the Friday and Saturday of Holy Week, when, so far as they could see, Jesus was gone. It was a time when all that they had ever felt of despair and discouragement and sadness and disappointment was heightened a hundred-fold. It must have struck them like a sharp pain, that there is this sinister and evil thing in the world to be reckoned with: and for all their optimism and cheerfulness, their Master was gone. " We thought that it was He Who should redeem Israel," were the forlorn words of the disappointed company.

But then came a third stage. It was a stage which reconciled the two first periods. There did not seem to be much relation between Galilee and Golgotha; but the empty tomb in the Arimathean garden was related to both. It brought a joy and an optimism far deeper than what they had known in the early days, but which gave new meaning to the messages and life of those days. It was closely connected with Golgotha, for without Golgotha there never could have been Resurrection. In a sense, it is an instance of the old idea of a thesis, then an antithesis, then a synthesis. Pre-Crucifixion Christianity was too ignorant of the darker side of life; Crucifixion-Christianity was too much drowned in that darker side; Post-Crucifixion Christianity gave to both their proper places.

Of course, historically, Post-Crucifixion Christianity knew greater power and liberation than any other period had known. They had seen a great light burn in Christ; they had seen that light extinguished on Good Friday. Now the light began to burn in themselves. " Did not our heart burn within us while He talked with us by the way? " The Christ without withdrew after a time: but the Christ within was realer than ever. The movement reassembled, the despair was gone, and led by this risen and reascended Lord, they went out to conquer the world. Not until after He was gone did He send the Spirit. The Spirit belongs to this third period. All along He had been working. We say every Sunday that it is the same Spirit who " spake by the prophets." But what the Christ had given before, of guidance and power and illumination, now the Spirit gave. There was no cessation of His activity, rather a quickening of it. And under that leadership kingdoms were won for Christ. It was a risen Christ Whom St. Paul saw and began to follow. And in his philosophy you will find him, again and again, dwelling upon the death of Christ and then upon the Resurrection and risen life and power of Christ. He knew that in what happened to Jesus, on the Cross and on Easter, was the solution for the problem of sin and the mystery of suffering. They constituted the great window upon the unplumbed mysteries of suffering and the vanquishment of it. This was the period of perhaps the greatest inward transformations of individuals; and these men found that the Lord Christ could do through them the same things that once He did for them.

Now: these three types are still found amongst

us to-day; and I would like to say some things to them and about them if any of them are here this morning.

The Pre-Crucifixion Christians are often interested in a moral ideal, and believe that the positive side ought to be emphasized. They do not pay very much attention to sin, and sometimes criticize us when we preach much about it. They believe Christianity to be a beautiful thing, as of course it is; and that all humanity is easily to be persuaded of Christianity without any reference to their own sins, as of course it is *not*. They want to hear about the love of God, and man's practical duty, and they want to find everybody sunny and bright, as of course we all do, but it cannot be done upon any but a much surer foundation than they have. These Pre-Crucifixion Christians are sometimes young and immature; they are sometimes very healthy, or else drugged with a philosophy which does not admit the existence of evil, which just means they have not faced some of the facts. They are sky-blue kind of people, like Pollyanna; sometimes lovable and interested in high things, but fledglings, spiritually young. They have not moved through some of the heavier experiences of life, and seen the weakness of their position, just as Simon Peter had not when he rebuked the Lord for calling attention to the coming of the Cross. One sometimes wishes the Pre-Crucifixion Christian were sufficient, that there were nothing else but the love of God and the duty of man to consider. One wishes that the man in the street, who asks us only to talk about certain practical considerations, were a good man to follow; but these people leave out something without which Christianity could never have held the hearts of men and women as it has. For life moves into its crucifixion-period, do what we will to prevent it: and God be merciful to those whose philosophy is of that rosy order which cannot be taken with them when they enter into the valley! The unutterable tragedy of those who have keyed themselves up to a false optimism, which does not work in the day of disaster, is one of the most dreadful fruits of the kind of belief which is running all through our world to-day, asking people to make believe the darker side is not there by not facing it. It *is* there, and it is coming to you some day, and to me. And I want a Christianity with a second period!

But there is another type of person, more initiated than the first, the Crucifixion-Christians of to-day. They see life so deeply dark with sin and sorrow and irony and pathos, such huge unfairnesses and such gross injustices that they stand forever in the shadow of humanity's cross. They know that simple morality is not enough, that it is idle to talk of the love of God without asking what the love of God means related to this vast spectacle of human misery. They know that you cannot go to men and women with this child's belief in the unalterable goodness of things, or without treating as real some of the losses and sorrows and tragedies through which they are called to go.

Anyone with forty years' experience will probably have come into this period some time since. Sometimes they are people who have themselves deeply suffered, been cut and bruised by life; and when they look at the whole thing they simply stand aghast and do not know what to make of it. They may be brave and cheery people on the outside: but inwardly they are baffled by life. Sometimes they are also very young people who assume that Christianity is all of the first order, simple and very serene; and they become vicarious skeptics, skeptics on account of other people whose miseries they see; and they go off to ponder and brood over a very moody philosophy which probably won't last long. Sometimes they are theological Christians who belong to this Crucifixion period: and their weakness consists of thinking that Christ did nothing else but die on a Cross and that all we must do is to accept a certain philosophy of that event, and we are Christians, without going any further by incorporating both the first and the third phases of historical Christianity into our whole faith. I do not wonder at these people. Life is sometimes desperately hard. I think it much better to face all these things, rather than to put your head into the sand and deny them, just because you don't want to believe them. But that is not enough: for those who see to this deeper level, need to see to a still deeper level before their minds can come to a rest with permanent satisfaction.

And, thank God, we have amongst us Post-Crucifixion Christians as well: people who see Christi-

anity in all its phases; who know the beauty of
ethical teaching and holy living and strong emphasis upon whatsoever is true and pure and of good
report; but who know also that this is not all we
have to face in life, and that the dark things in
life need interpreting as much as the bright, and
that any faith which is to keep hold of us all
through our natures must face both sides of the
picture. In their Christian *faith* they believe, not
only in the human Jesus of Nazareth, but in the
divine Christ of Cæsarea Philippi, and in the
human and divine Christ of Gethsemane and Calvary, Who both lived for our edification and died
for our sins, and then rose again that we might
know the reality of eternal life. In their Christian
practise, they believe in the moral principles and
want to apply them; but they know also that our
deepest need is not for more instruction but for
more inspiration, not for more knowledge of what
to do, but for some liberated power in putting all
that into effect; and that there is a power in the
Cross which was not in the uncrucified Christ, a
power in the sent Spirit which was to be of greater
service to humanity than even the Christ Who
walked our earth. They know something of the
joy of living which was the search of the pagan,
but came to its full flower in Christ. They know
also something of the sorrow of living which has
been part of us all from the beginning of time, but
came to its fullest interpretation in the Cross of
Christ. And so when it comes to dealing with people, they would say something like this: the kind

of life we want to see you live is the kind of life Jesus lived when He walked in Galilee and taught and worked and healed and served—that is the ideal of life. You all agree to that kind of living, and say with your hearts that it is the finest kind the world ever saw. But the thing which keeps humanity back from it is the sin of men's hearts, and the sorrow which wrecks men's faith without some interpretation which brings comfort and hope. Therefore you cannot leave out the Cross in your Christianity, as you cannot leave it out of your life. But the harmony of these two things only comes when you accept the risen Christ in what St. Paul calls " the power of His resurrection," and go forward into the new period of Christian living. The risen Christ was not quite in His old body; and whatever that change involved, it meant more freedom for Him than He ever knew before. The ascended Christ was entirely removed from their sight: but when He had ascended, the Spirit came, and men knew for a certainty that they had not lost their Christ at all, but that from the glory of His ascended life He can and does pour down upon us broadcast and everywhere power and joy that very few understood before, through the liberation of the Spirit.

And so it is that, going up and down in the common highways, through the routine of a well-ordered and unselfishly planned life, or the steady loyalty of a growingly deep relationship, or the pursuit of an aim which when attained will make life sweeter and happier for someone else, through duty done and through the slow development of a larger love, we shall continue to find the Christ drawing near to us, in unexpected places—the Christ Who took our life just where He found it, and cared enough to live it all and to give to it all His own interpretation—the Christ of the roadway, the Christ of the rejection, and the Christ of the resurrection—and we shall know Him, and when we turn to look into a human face, there to find confirmation of our experience in the experience of another, we shall say as they said of old, " Did not our heart burn within us, while He talked with us by the way? "

O LORD JESUS CHRIST, we pray Thee to lead us into a full interpretation of all that Thou hast done amongst us. Give us a whole Gospel. Rouse us where we have been resting content with half the truth. Keep us from blindness and self-deception. Teach us to see all the sorrow of our life and all the need of mankind caught up into Thy Cross: and to know that there the world may find its medicine. Come to us to-day, risen Lord, and send us forth from Thy house knowing that Thou hast met us in the way, and our hearts have burned with recognition and with thankfulness. We ask it in Thy Name. Amen.

IX

THE MEANING OF THE CROSS

"For if, while we were enemies, we were reconciled to God through the death of His Son, much more, being reconciled, shall we be saved through His life; and not only so, but we also rejoice in God through our Lord Jesus Christ, through Whom we have now received the reconciliation."
—ROMANS 5: 10–11.

THIS age is not much in the mood for theology. The best of theology is always the explanation of an experience or a well-authenticated phenomenon. It is unfortunately terribly possible for men to cling to the form of explanation long after they have ceased to have the experience. And so it has been with all of the great Christian doctrines: men have been holding to them and preaching them long after the time when they were really experiencing them in their own lives. We have done it with the Holy Spirit, we have done it with the divinity of Jesus, we have notably done it with the Atonement. And finding men saying dry things about these conceptions which ought to pulsate with sheer importance, we have tended to throw theology into the discard, and to be done with it.

Popular preachers have taken up the cry, and make a cheap appeal to their hearers by decrying theology in the name of freedom and intellectual emancipation. It reveals a poverty of spiritual experience, in some cases, and a want of the very intellectual dignity which they profess. Theology is ordered thought about the Father of our spirits, and the issues of our own eternal lives. If anything matters, that matters. If anything is worth serious intellectual attention, that is.

To-day I ask you to try to think through with me something of the meaning of the Cross. I know of nothing in all Christianity which is more difficult to understand, in some of its aspects. There are theories about it which are unintelligible or immoral. Nobody has said the final word about it. But as I read the New Testament I am profoundly impressed by the fact that St. Paul had a far deeper experience of the Cross than contemporary Christianity knows much about. There were those who, a generation or two ago, knew the same power of the Cross. We have lost something, and we need to recover it.

Let me say at once that it is not the *spirit* of the Cross which is our great lack. I doubt if there has ever been so much outpoured generosity in the world's history as there is to-day. We sometimes speak of the meaning of those who do not give sacrificially: but there are many who do— give of their time and their money and their energy and their very lives for the relief and happiness of other human beings. But this was not the chief note in the apostolic emphasis on the Cross. They felt brought into a wholly new relationship to God by the reconciliation of Christ: and we can well afford to spend some time trying to understand what they meant by it.

The first and most obvious meaning of the Cross was the consummate moral earnestness of Jesus Himself. Again and again He predicted it as the only natural outcome of the kind of life He was living, with its terrific challenge to men. He would hear of no small devices of human safety. He walked straight where His conscience led Him; and the storm gathered, as He said it would. And He went through it unflinchingly. This is not the great meaning of the Cross: but it is the one all men can see, the skeptical, the stupid, the wise, the little children. All men are arrested by courage which will not evade the risks involved in duty. This links the Cross down into our common life, and makes it part of all fine and noble living.

But this alone would never have made of the Cross a supreme element in the Christian religion. Socrates died nobly, and Lincoln, and a host of other lofty-souled men. There is nothing here which has to do with the everlasting destiny of humanity, nothing to call a " reconciliation " with God.

We cannot get to a deeper significance of the Cross until we consider the problem with which the Cross had to deal. So far as it concerns us directly, that problem was our human estrangement from God. There may be a cosmic significance to the Cross which we cannot apprehend. St. John speaks of the " sin of the cosmos."

There may be a wider existence of evil than in human sin: and God may have vast concerns beyond His relation to us. Jesus said, " Be of good cheer: I have overcome the cosmos." But we can only touch the fringes of the Cross where it applies to us, in the relation between God and ourselves. And we have been drawn away from Him. St. Paul says bluntly " we were enemies." He does not say that God was our enemy, but that we were God's enemies. That is to say, we had rejected His way for our own. We were fighting against His way. All sin is that. And my sin has put a distance between God and me. What was true of the race, is also true of every member of it. We all go through disobedience and fall, and there never was a greater allegory of spiritual fact in the world than the story of the expulsion from the Garden of Eden. Any man with the slightest spark of imagination can trace a parallel in his own life; and not one but many.

The fact is that I sin. I deliberately sin. With my eyes open, with my mind perfectly aware of God's opposition to what I am about to do, with a will unstruggling against evil but consciously choosing it instead, I have many a time and oft chosen my way as against God's. And that means that there are moral lapses in me for which I can never hope to atone. I have nothing in myself to plead. It makes a gap between myself and the Ideal which I am powerless to bridge. It distances me from the All-holy God. And I cannot climb or crawl back across that distance.

Even the love of God cannot make me innocent again. I must leave that forever. The Prodigal in the far country never can be as though he had stayed at home. There is but one thing left: forgiveness.

All through the Gospels the forgiveness of God is held out as free and immediate to anyone who repents. There are no further or other conditions. To prodigal or harlot, to Pharisee or sinner, to those old in sin or those who first offend, forgiveness is extended on the sole condition of repentance. That is the glory of the Gospel, and its power of bringing hope to those whom the world has given up. It means the indiscriminate love of God, scattered broadcast across the face of the earth for all who will receive it with penitence. God is never an enemy, but always, and everywhere, a lover.

But sin would not be sin if God could lightly deal with it. God hates sin. It is nothing which He can merely obliterate, as we wipe a chalk-mark off a board. Sin is not only the disappointment of His love: sin is the outrage of His holiness. There is a real antagonism of God to sin which no easy theory of God's love can evade. And when we draw a distinction between sin and sinner, we are seeking shelter for ourselves: for we make sin, and there is no sin apart from us. Therefore there is a real antagonism of God toward us. His love yearns for us, but His righteousness demands satisfaction also. Free forgiveness, therefore, would be immoral if it were lightly given. Therefore there must be something to manifest the cost of forgiveness to God.

Only God, therefore, can deal with sin. He must contrive to do for us what we have lost the power to do for ourselves. I hear men say that they will slough off sin in their onward march toward perfection. It seems to me childish. What will they do about the past, about wilful wrong that has involved other people, and certain kinds of sin the whole consequences of which can never be humanly atoned for? What is going to make up for all " the days desolate and wasted years "? Nothing will do but for God Himself to stoop in ministrant condescension and good-will, and take these things upon Himself, and carry them for us.

Only God can deal with His own wrath against sin. The meaning of reconciliation is, not that God was moved by the entreaties of repentant humanity to make us as though we had not sinned: it is that God, in the Atonement, voluntarily and of Himself put away all estrangement on His side, and by a colossal act of self-humbling and sin-bearing, made peace possible. Holiness and love met in the Cross.

Men talk glibly to-day about the love of God. We think of Him as practically-minded, a sort of good-natured Chairman of the committee of the cosmos, who can always be depended upon to dispense with parliamentary rules and give us a chance to speak for ourselves. There is an appalling amount of sinning on the part of people who have learned to expect God to forgive them.

We literally take the love of God for granted. And the terrible thing is that the love of God is there—just as free as we heedless and thankless human beings assume that it is—and we can go on sinning and keep on coming back to Him just as long as we care to do it, and He will still be there waiting for us.

You can do just two things with that kind of love—you can go on abusing it and making use of it—or you can fall back abashed in the presence of it and be forever a new creature because of it. You can accept it as your due, as what you expected God to do for you, as your right—or you can fall utterly prostrate before it in gratitude. It is an immense thing for us to expect the Holy God to condescend to us, to be concerned about us, to offer forgiveness to us. The other day I sat with a man who is a modern saint, in a home he keeps for destitute men. One of them had complained that God had not answered his prayer. " Why should He answer your prayer? " asked this saint. " You have served the devil most of your life—why should God take any notice of you at all? " That sounds like harsh doctrine: but until we have a fresh vision of the Majesty of God, and get some more of that kind of religion, we shall never extricate ourselves from the toils of a merely ethical religion. We have got a smooth religion of duty because we have lost the sense of *debt*. We talk about the love of God as though we owned it. We ride in it proudly, as if we bought and paid for it. We have forgotten the cost to God of forgiveness which is the beginning of His love for us. The Cross was raised on Calvary's hill to prevent men from ever forgetting that love costs God His life.

The deepest meaning of the Cross is that God made reconciliation for us with Himself. We shall never understand the Cross until we understand the horror of human sin and the holiness of God. It is something which God did for us, nothing we did for ourselves. The very beginning of our religion is nothing we do, it is something done for us—a gift to us. Grace comes first, then character. Salvation first, then service. The ordinary mood of cheerful Christians is generally one of trying to help God to remake His world: in that attitude we live as happy and industrious Christians. But that is not the deepest note in our relation to God. I suspect that the deepest note in human love is not service but gratitude—it is when one marvels that *such* a person can possibly care for him—when the relationship seems all one-sided, with oneself all the receiver and the other all the giver. One's response to that kind of love is to do all that one can—but that seems negligible and utterly incommensurate with what has been received.

Our most serious problem to-day is not, I think, outbreaking sin, but pride. Better drunkenness and violence and crime, with honesty enough to call them by their names, than the state of mind which thanks God we are not as other men are. We have left the Cross almost entirely out of mod-

ern Christianity because our attitude toward
Christ is one of standing beside Him to help Him.
It is presumptuous. It is full of pride. We need
desperately some pride-destroying element in our
religion—something which will provoke pride to
repent. Pride avoids common sin, and is compla-
cent: or pride commits ordinary sin, and does not
call it sin. What can make sin appear " exceeding
sinful " ? Nothing but the exhibition of suffering
love. If that does not break the pride of humanity, nothing can. It is God's utmost to shake us
out of our independence.

Not only can we count upon the love of God at
all times: but He has sealed and demonstrated that
love in the Atonement of the Cross. As St. Paul
says, " we have received the reconciliation." The
reconciliation is as much a spiritual fact as the
estrangement from God. Through Christ we do
" have access " to the Father. He has cleared
away that cloud, and we have stood in a new relation to God ever since He did. I cannot tell you
all that the Cross meant in the heart of God. I am
sure that the Cross is more than the death of a
Good Man. I am sure that it is steadily altering
the attitude of the world toward God. I believe
that, where love and holiness met together, it altered God's attitude toward the world. He always
loved the world: but holiness required sacrifice for
the sin of the world. Through Christ the holiness
of God was satisfied. And the way to the Father
has been an open way all these subsequent centuries.

That is something of the meaning of the Cross. We shall find other meanings on Good Friday. If we read Romans and Galatians this Holy Week, we shall find something of what St. Paul believed about the Cross. We stand here to-day surrounded by the sunshine of an unlimited and unmerited forgiveness. God went beyond anything we really deserved, and gave us instead what we needed for restoration. We have been literally loosed from our sins.

What shall we do in the presence of so great love? " Beloved, if God *so* loved us, we also ought to love one another." The forgiven must forgive. We cannot keep the reconciliation which has been given to us, unless we become infinite extensions of that reconciliation into the world. We pray every day that God will forgive us " as we forgive those who trespass against us." We dare ask of Him no more love than we are willing to give back ourselves to the world. The mark and pledge of a redeemed spirit is that we shall become ourselves as forgiving as God.

Let us pray:

Look, Father, look on His anointed face,
  And only look on us as found in Him;
Look not on our misusings of Thy grace,
  Our prayer so languid, and our faith so dim;
For lo! between our sins and their reward,
  We set the Passion of Thy Son our Lord.   Amen.

X

THE CROSS IN HUMAN RELATIONS

"He was wounded for our transgressions, He was bruised for our iniquities: the chastisement of our peace was upon Him; and with His stripes we are healed."—ISAIAH 53: 5.

I ASK you to think with me of the practical meaning of the Cross. We all know that the triumph of our Lord in Jerusalem on that first Palm Sunday was short-lived and included but a small portion of the population. Those who acclaimed Him were the Galilæans and His friends: the populace of Jerusalem never accepted Him. They doubted Him that first Palm Sunday, and through the week their sullenness grew into open hostility. Already the Cross looms as the outcome of His " setting His face to go toward Jerusalem."

More and more one feels that Jesus said more and accomplished more through the Cross than anywhere else. Whenever the Christian religion grows profound, it becomes preoccupied with the Cross. Every generation contributes something to the interpretation of it, but fails to say the last word. The Cross is a never-failing fountain of Christian inspiration and thought. There remains more in it than we have yet discovered.

To-day I am going to give you my own interpretation of the Cross, and then try to relate the principle of it to present life. I believe that the Cross really understood would revolutionize our human relationships. I believe that I have got hold of a truth which, if we could lay hold of it as the working-principle of our lives, would actually make Christians of us all.

Now as I read the Gospel of Jesus Christ, I get no light upon the metaphysical question of the origin of sin and evil. Jesus treats them as present facts, to be dealt with practically and not theoretically. And if Jesus reflects God's mind toward human problems, God too must take a practical attitude toward a rebellious, disobedient, wayward, sinning humanity.

What possible attitudes were open to Him?

There are three possible attitudes for God to take, as I see it.

He might repudiate human sin, turn His back upon humanity, and ignore us forever. He could close the ways to Him, draw down the veil, and leave us to rue our sins alone. We never sin without warning. Something in us cries out against it every time we do it. Most of us know, even in our sins, that they are an offense toward God. It would have been only a strict justice, only a giving us our deserts, if God had taken that attitude toward us. We are impotent in His hands, and He might have dealt with us according to our deserts.

Or He might have condoned our sins. He might have said, " Poor, pitiful humanity, groping for

the light, living in the dark! They cannot be expected to do any better. They are doing the best
they can. Their wills are so weak, their equip-
ment is so poor, their light so flickering. The only
thing to do is to fling forgiveness broadcast and
free, wipe out old scores, and hold nothing against
anybody." That looks like the quickest solution,
until you remember that life has a purpose, which
is the development of human character through
struggle and moral discrimination—and then its
shallow inadequacy lies clear on the surface.

There was a third possible attitude of God: He
might absorb our sins. It was a profound insight
into this solution which made Isaiah, in his inspired fifty-third chapter, look forward to the Redeemer and say, "He was wounded for our
transgressions, He was bruised for our iniquities:
the chastisement of our peace was upon Him; and
with His stripes we are healed."

Now may I try to analyze with you something of
what the principle of absorption really means?

To absorb the sins of another, it is necessary
first to enter fully into his situation, see it through
his eyes, to begin where he is without asking any
questions about why the past has been what it was.
"Should not have been" is no part of the vocabu-
lary of absorption. When Jesus found the woman
taken in adultery, He first accepted her as a person, utterly without regard to whether she had
sinned or not. He took her part as a human being, showing no sign of what He thought of her
sin. No redemption was possible until she knew

that He stood with her. The first move was identification. The Pharisees wanted Him to repudiate:
probably the woman wanted Him to condone; but
He wanted to absorb. First He must get into such
a relation with the woman that He could absorb.
He saw her sin quite as clearly as the Pharisees,
but He did not judge *her* as they did. This means
that the redeemer, human or divine, must begin by
facing facts about us, without pronouncing judgment upon them. He must take us as we are, and
begin with us as he finds us. He must put himself
on our level, not by sinning as we sin, but by identifying himself with us through absolute sympathy.
In His general relation to humanity, God did this
through the Incarnation of Jesus Christ in human
flesh, living our life with no privileges or exemp-
tions, subject fully to all that we experience and
suffer.

But then, having made known that his attitude
toward the offender is one of love, sympathy, identification, the redeemer must make known his attitude toward the offense. He must challenge. He
must give some sign, not only of the tenderness of
his heart, but of the justice of his mind. Silence
persisted in too long would make the offender feel
that he repudiated, if it seemed a sullen silence: or
that he condoned, if it were a tolerant silence. He
must indicate his own frank estimate of the situation, if he is to go beyond a sympathy which may
in the last analysis, be only morally debilitating.
And so, when the Pharisees had removed their
miserable carcases to a safe distance, He again

solidified Himself through repeated sympathy with the woman before Him: "Neither do I condemn thee," but He added the word which let her know just what He thought of the offense, "Go, and sin no more." The Pharisees did not hear that, He would not give their vice-hounding imaginations the satisfaction of hearing it: they were out to repudiate, and He was out to absorb. They wanted to judge her for sinning: He wanted her to stop sinning. There comes a time in dealing with a person in real sin when we must in all sympathy let them know what we see and how we feel, in our deepest, most impersonal, most concerned moments. It is the truth that makes men free. And the truth will win its way by its own self-luminous clarity and its freedom from personal judgingness. God first made us see, in Christ, that He is one with us; and then He made us see that He is different from us. He made His identification with us known through Christ, and then through the same Christ He put forth a Gospel which analyzes us to the core. He made Himself our best Friend, and then He told us just what He thought. We so often fail to redeem because we talk about the offender to someone else, or let someone else talk about him to us. Jesus said it all to our faces.

Now because of the fact that "the truth hurts," we all tend to regard home-truths as "charges," and the "faithful wounds of a friend" as accusatory, no matter how completely the redeemer has first proven his identification with us by love.

When he speaks, we think that he speaks harshly, and call him a judge when he is only an honest friend. Sometimes we have the grace and insight to accept the truth when it is spoken; thereby saving both the redeemer and ourselves from unpredictable suffering: it is a staggering thought to imagine how different the course of human development might have been, had humanity known the day of its visitation and been disposed to listen to Jesus Christ, instead of to get rid of Him. But our usual course is retaliation. And to this the true redeemer makes no reply. "As a sheep before his shearers is dumb, so openeth He not His mouth." Isaiah saw all this long before the Redeemer actually came. The redeemer is defenceless. He has no weapon but the truth. When men complicate the truth, or deny it, he has no other resort. Force has no place in his armoury, for force takes no conviction to the heart. The truth must make its own way in its own time. Redemptiveness means the free gift of our best: if this is trampled on and we seek to defend ourselves, we fail. We cannot prove the rightness of what we say by anything but the convicting power of its own rightness. The redeemer may explain himself, as sometimes Jesus answered His questioners: or he may, if so led, leave the truth to carry its own conviction, unbuttressed by further human confirmation, as Jesus maintained unbroken silence before Pilate. If we speak further, it must be to add light, not heat: if we remain silent, it must be loving and without sulkiness. The redemptive attitude can make no demands about the future, as it asked no questions about the past. It cannot spread its love and expect obedience in return. It puts the case, but cannot extort promises of amendment because of its own unselfish outlay. It can do nothing about its own rewards. It risks everything in a great gamble that the truth is self-evident to every mind, and that human beings at bottom crave the best. Beyond this, it has no self-protective devices.

Now nothing so much maddens the world as actual, visible redemptiveness of this kind. If we are mellow and open, we are overcome by it. But if we stiffen our backs at all, we feel the implied judgment upon our competitive and self-seeking motives. And the world gets busy to show up the folly of this sort of attitude and its " unworkabil-ity " in the practical realm. The individual in whom redemptiveness is most incarnated will re-ceive the most unremitting blows of the world's scorn and hatred. Jesus before Pilate is the su-preme image of this; but all His saints, and the wise of other folds, instance the same truth: Soc-rates drinking his hemlock, and Gandhi in prison for his own redemptiveness. The farther one goes with this, the more likely is it to end in one's own destruction. The mob on Calvary said more than they knew when they cried, " He saved others, Himself He cannot save." The redeemer may be burnt up in the fires of his own absorbing zeal. The Cross of Christ is simply this principle found at its zenith, in classic and historic instance.

There the stung and convicted sin of man, chan-
nelled and concentrated through the cowardice of
Pilate and the cruelty of the crowd, broke full
upon His naked and defenceless Head. All the
deepest dye and essence of all the distilled wrong
of the world was poured out in towering wrath
upon Him. " He was wounded for our transgressions, He was bruised for our iniquities: the chastisement of our peace was upon Him; and with
His stripes we are healed." It was not the suffering of Jesus which saved us: it was the way He
carried us on His heart and went to Calvary for
us. This is the utmost to which love can go. This
is love—disinterested, redemptive, sin-absorbing
love—without limit.

Now we often think that the great danger in
thinking about the Cross is to put it in the category of ordinary human sacrifice, but I think that
it is rather making of the Cross an event so unique
that we come to feel that we, being finite and
sinful, cannot even begin to follow in its track.
Everything about Jesus has a farther-end which is
mysterious and unfathomable: but it has also a
nearer-end which is useful and practical. Only
One can be the Sin-Bearer of the world: but His
great act must have radiations and reflections in
all our common life, which must come by way of
the Christians.

I ask you, therefore, to lift up all your human
relationships into the light of these three principles, and see under which they fall. We have but
three ways in which to deal with the wrongs of

óthers, as God had but three ways to deal with our wrongs. We can only repudiate, or condone, or absorb.

We can turn our backs on those who wrong us, or wrong others known to us, and say that it is all an outrage and shut them out of our lives. The brief and final phrase for this is, " I'm through." I know a man to whose house a guest came for twenty years. One day that guest said something to the man which was true, but unwelcome, and never again was he asked to that house, nor was he given any explanation, or chance to talk the matter out. There is the principle of repudiation in a nut-shell. It withdraws to a distance and sits down in judgment. It usurps the function of God, which even He did not care to exercise, of judging without mercy. It assumes in the judge the clean heart, the moteless, beamless eye, the absolute attitude, which of course none of us possesses. It damns itself by its own sterility, its finality, its powerlessness to better matters in any respect, or to do anything further for the offender.

Or we can be lenient, and, as we love to call it these days, " tolerant." We quote to ourselves the French proverb, of doubtful ethics, that to know everything is to pardon everything. And we pride ourselves on our capacity to understand: it is the principle of identification gone to seed. I know a Christian woman of understanding and sympathy so great that she is always helping people to lay down their faults to incurable, inherited temperament, identifying herself with them at the expense of principle and objective truth, and sending them out from her convinced of her saintly sympathy and their own virtual innocence. This gives to her a reputation for kindheartedness which would be grateful to us all. But an attitude which gives people further excuse for remaining as they are is, at best, a doubtful one. Sometimes false science, and false religion give us further comfort in this direction. One says to us that we are biologically only animals, and our best efforts produce only imperceptible advance. The other declares that there is no such thing as sin, it is only " error ": I lose my temper with a fellow-worker, and I am not guilty, but only unfortunate and undeveloped. This is an elaborate philosophy of let-down. Whatever deflates our moral responsibility slowly disintegrates the very possibility of progress, and is the counsel of hopelessness.

But there is the larger, more difficult, more expensive course open to us, of the absorption of human wrong-doing. It begins with identification. For God, identification meant condescension: but for us it means the humility of conscious oneness with sinners in their sin. Obviously, we ill fit the rôle of redeemer. Only the One Perfect can be the ideal redeemer. For us, innocence is gone, and perfection is not come. We must therefore take our sins consciously with us, when we set out to redeem, and let them perform their one earthly service of usefulness,—that of identifying us, beyond escape or forgetting, with those who sin.

Then we must move on to learning the facts,

and understanding the situation just as it is. Psychiatrist, priest or wise lay-adviser, all are bound to do this. We must redeem precisely what we find, not something else. Optimism looks foolishly above the facts, and thinks to get along without them; pessimism looks foolishly below them, and thinks them insurmountable: but wisdom looks at them. Genuine redemption is always inductive, pragmatic, scientific at this end. As facts come out, from cumulative evidence an intelligent diagnosis is made without showing criticalness, distrust or final decision. Here is where Jesus' " Judge not " comes in. He cannot possibly mean, " Do not form an estimate ": He must mean, " Do not consider an estimate as an end: your end is to redeem." We are not finally interested in the allocation of guilt, except in so far as it has practical consequences in amendment, for it is a theoretical consideration: we are interested only in salvation, which is a practical matter.

We have already said that the truth makes men free, and the truth will win its own way through its own self-evident luminousness. It is refreshing, life-giving to men and women spoon-fed on flattery and complimentary humbug. The earnest, the sincere, the unsophisticated will often welcome the light thus revealed, take it, and begin to live by it. On the other hand, the servant is not above his Lord: what they gave Him, they will sometimes give us also. The great redeemers have always suffered, been persecuted, paid with their pains, and sometimes with their lives, for the unspeakable

privilege of sharing with God in redemption. I
know of none of them, historic or to-day alive, who
have not somewhere undergone their counterpart
of the Wilderness, Gethsemane and Calvary. We
may identify a little, or condone a little: but when
we do, we are patch-workers in human souls.
Those who go through with it, and make men
really new in God, suffer. " Without shedding of
blood, there is no remission." But the person in
whom the principle of redemption has become a
rooted attitude expects defeat, uses it, understands
it, knows that defeat can no more be defeated, but
only waits lowly in the dust for its own vindica-
tion.

Now this, it seems to me, is the Cross in common life. This is the way in which suffering love
goes on redeeming forever. By this means, I say
it reverently, you and I may be " wounded for
their transgressions, and bruised for their iniquities: the chastisement of their peace may be upon
us, and with our stripes, they may be healed."

I feel quite certain that it is our failure to take
this principle of absorption, as against hard repudiation, or soft condonment, into our common life
that makes so many people say we Christians are
not Christians at all. Now let us face some of our
commonest relationships in this light.

First, our own families, those who, out of all the
world by choice and by blood are our own. We
may find ourselves married to someone who never
has learned elementary self-control, and is con-
stantly miserable and making others miserable, by

explosions of temper or wilfulness. Our child grows up with some obnoxious defect which annoys us in private and shames us in public. Our parents may seem slow to us, or out-of-date. Now here we can repudiate, and express it by judgment and criticism. We may hide our repudiation, yet keep it in our hearts, never really being one with them in bearing their defect or helping them to master it, never expecting them to be freed from it, merely enduring it with them. Or we may condone the fault, gloss it over, never mention it, and like a physical malady, make the best of it; yet this never means any progress. But suppose we begin to absorb, treat their sin not as a fate but as a problem, get under their sins, and actually carry with them the burden of discomfort and remorse, forgetful of anything that *we* suffer. Some day we must by identification melt down the walls entirely, till there is honest flow between them and us of just how we feel. We must be careful never to obtrude self-interest and the protection of our rights. We must look for nothing less than the whole redemption of this whole personality, seeing them afresh, not as family problem, but as potential miracle of grace. Anything less as a prospect means mere human tinkering and management, full of dynamite and often the cause of irreparable breach. It takes constructive patience which " beareth all things, believeth all things, hopeth all things." Absorption will mean a large serenity which speaks seldom, prays much and never nags, large with the hope that is born of prayer. What different homes we should have were this always our principle!

Then take our attitude toward other Christians: especially those who have taken a more courageous course than we, and are still found not without fault, and perhaps are even fallen by the wayside. We usually take this, do we not, as an index that our cautious way is proved the better? We stand apart from them, declare conversion emotional excitement only, condemn " fanaticism " (by which we mean practically anything that would dig us out of our lethargy), and comfort ourselves with the reflection that all growth is slow, forgetful that rust and rot is also slow. Or else we condone by being broad-minded, calling human nature uncertain, excusing their back-slidings because we cannot heal them, say they are probably doing the best they can, inexpensively " God bless them," and let them go their way. How much better were it to absorb their failings! Then we should remember that if one member of Christ suffer, all the others suffer also: if one fall, all fall; if this man fall, *I* fall with him. There would be no standing apart and detached criticism: the same look of disappointment would be on our faces as was on Christ's when He saw Peter beginning to weaken, and such as I have seen many a time in the eyes of the real identified redeemers—and so different from that loveless, faithless, hopeless, godless look of " What's the use—I knew you couldn't hold him! ", which I have seen so often on the face of the onlooking repudiators or con-

doners, some of them loudly calling themselves
Christians! So easy to throw stones, so hard to
carry the load with the " devil's penitents "! So
utterly inexpensive to say it all proves a theory,
or disproves one, while the life is gone for want of
enough human backing to keep him from spiritual
loneliness and suicide! So cheap also to condone,
and chart for human beings the safer way of timid
resolve and generous excuse: but this does not lift
nor change him! It is all so demanding of patience and faith and forgivingness and life-blood
to worry with these weak, intractable, wavering,
sinful people. But who are we to talk in this fashion? Are not we, in God's sight, just as stubborn
and unsteady as they? If God bled for us, we
ought also to bleed for the brethren!

And again, think of those who have definitely
wronged us, or wished us evil. For the moment,
let us assume that the affair is all of their own
making and the guilt on their side, though you
know as well as I that it probably isn't. Now
what shall we do? If we repudiate, we shall an-
nounce their guilt, drive them away, and be finished with them forever: it will inflate our ego and
give us topic for much talk. If we condone, it
may remove the hardness from our own hearts, but
it will not change the offender: the important thing
here is not what he has done to us or to others, it
is that *he is the kind of man who does that kind
of thing*. Jesus would try to absorb, I believe.
And here is where His principle of non-resistance
comes in: it is the principle of non-repudiation.

"If thine enemy hunger, feed him." Get into touch with him. See him as a soul and a life. Forget your grievance. We are set to redeem. We must get under that man's sins, carry them with him, not because they bother us, but because they bother him, and wall him off from full relation with God and his fellows. This may lay us open to all sorts of things to be said by him and by others: that we have no self-respect, are weak, are admitting the fault in ourselves. No redeemer seeks to be understood: he seeks to redeem. To redeem he must absorb. To absorb he must identify himself with the wrong-doer. Some day that kind of love melts down walls like candle-grease, and brings his pride as low as yours has been. And as both of you stand honest before God, ready to make amends, you will find that you know what Jesus meant when He said, "Love your enemies: pray for them which despitefully use you and persecute you." And he will know how another can be "wounded for our transgressions, and bruised for our iniquities; how the chastisement of our peace can be upon Him, and with His stripes we can be healed."

There is not time to go on as I would, and relate this principle to all the manifold relationships of life where you know, as I do, that it would work a veritable miracle. You know, too, that the only one great obstacle to living this out is our pride: it is a difficult course, but it is a clear one. I ask you to roll those three words round and round in your mind. Repudiation and condonement will turn like smooth stones: absorption will catch and tear the sides of your mind, recalling to you, as it does to me, a hundred misspent opportunities, showing me why I failed here and here, and how I ought to proceed.

This is Holy Week. Our Saviour, in such a spirit as we but dimly feel after if haply we may find it, was this week " wounded for our transgressions, and bruised for our iniquities: the chastisement of our peace was upon Him; and with His stripes we are healed." I ask you to think with me all this Holy Week of what we must do to make the principle of absorption the essence and aim of our life, and to make the adjustments and decisions which this requires.

So may God bring us through Good Friday to Easter this year, having learned what mean " the fellowship of His sufferings " and the " glory of His resurrection."

XI

OUR NEED OF CHRIST'S CROSS

"For if the blood of goats and bulls, and the ashes of a heifer sprinkling them that have been defiled, sanctify unto the cleanness of the flesh: how much more shall the blood of Christ, Who through (the) eternal spirit offered Himself without blemish unto God, cleanse your conscience from dead works to serve the living God?"—HEBREWS 9: 13–14.

ORDINARILY we consider the Cross of Christ in the season of Lent and Good Friday, when it recurs in the round of the church year. We are reminded of it whenever we go to the Holy Communion, which is a "perpetual memory of that His precious death and sacrifice." We feel that the Cross stands behind the Christian experience, seals it with a great sacrifice, and lends itself as the characteristic symbol of Christianity.

But is this enough place to give to the Cross? In all the writings of St. Paul, and in all the deepest experience of Christian believers from that day till now, the Cross has not been one among many elements in the Christian faith. It has been absolutely and uniquely central. As Christ was the essence of God, localized where we could behold Him in one life, the Cross was the essence of Christ, where we could, as it were, behold Him in one act.

Here, in one vast, acute, representative item, we find the Gospel. So it is that Dr. Denney, one of the great Presbyterian theologians of the Cross, called the Atonement "Christianity in brief." Here, then, is not merely a piece of inherited dogma from past ages: here is something which for thousands of people who have taken it into their lives, has spelled more strength, more thankfulness, more surety, and more blessedness. Here is something which the simplest can remember from the symbol of the Cross itself, made either in wood or in gesture; and something which the wisest may ponder in an endless attempt to fathom the mystery of the love of God.

Now the Christian Church has been guilty at times of creating a formula about the Cross, and telling people to swallow that formula, and they would be saved. That kind of obscurantism can no longer win the favour of honest people. Unless we can see that there is intellectual reasonableness, or practical usefulness, in the holding of a belief, we will not accept it upon the say-so of tradition and authority. We admit that there may be an element of mystery, as there is concerning many things in which we believe and which we use every day: but unless we can catch that mystery by either the intellectual or practical hems, we are inclined to let it go. I have heard much effusive talk about the Cross from conservative Christians: but when I asked them what they meant, they put me off by phrases which they had not investigated, and which made only nonsense. Clearly they had not given the matter serious intellectual consideration, though I often recognized that they had hold of a great reality.

Now the need of a Cross at all arises out of the fact of our estrangement from God. That is a fact to any who see straight. Humanity is just exactly like the prodigal in the parable: we are out in the far country, away from the Father, with homesickness in our hearts. We know both where we are, and where we belong. Now, then, how can that distance be reduced? There must be repentance on our part, and forgiveness on God's.

Let me try to deal with the question of divine forgiveness. No theory of reconciliation between God and man is admissible which does not begin with the proposition that God is always and primarily Perfect Love. Any doctrine which regards God as needing to be appeased or coaxed round to kind-heartedness is immoral and un-Christian. We must remember, also, that forgiveness does not pertain to one special act, but to the whole personality as involved in that act: what it looks toward is a restored relationship. The broken relation is not that between a prisoner in the dock, and his judge: there is no relation there except one of temporary discipline. It is that between a son in the house, and his father: where the relation is organic. God will not, cannot, un-son us: He is love and He made us to be the objects of His love. But, so long as we persist in sin, there is a genuine antagonism which we have set up against God. We are fond of saying that God " hates the sin, and loves the sinner," which is true; but our sin comes out of our will: and the will is the citadel of the self. God can only love us sinning, in spite of our sin. Such part of us as is sinning is opposed to God: *and God is opposed to us.* It would frankly let us off easily and demoralize us to be forgiven outright. We must be made to see the outrage of sin against the holiness of God. And God can make that plain to us in either of two ways: by inflicting suffering upon us, or by manifesting the suffering which He endures through our alienation of ourselves. Being loving, He could not choose the former: He took the latter. And it is the Cross which, by showing what sin costs God, safeguards His righteousness while He forgives sin. The Cross was not Jesus' willing sacrifice of Himself in the light of which God decided to be merciful instead of harsh: the Cross is the uncovering of the heart of God in plain face of all men, that we might see in the divine heart both limitless love and majestic holiness. The Cross is the sign of God's forgiveness, and of its cost to Him. It both woos and condemns us. It calls, and it repels. Mercy and truth are met together: righteousness and peace have kissed each other.

What, now, is to bring about repentance in us? This is the other side of the condition to be fulfilled. We may think that fear would have produced it: but the repentance which comes about through fear still has self at its center, and is concerned with its own protection. We might repent, like the Prodigal, because of the unhappy conse-

quences of sin, which make us see that we have
been on the wrong track. But let us look deeper:
what is the heart of our impenitence? Not the
common sins, of sloth or impurity or crooked dealing, but something which underlies and includes
them all: self-sufficiency and the independence of
God—that is, for the Christian, the major sin of
all. It is pride par excellence, to try to get along
without God. If God is to produce repentance in
us, He must go for our pride. Now there is only
one thing in this world which can deflate pride,
and that is suffering love. Opposing pride cannot
do it, judgment cannot do it, nothing which is hard
or similar can do it: only something which is gentle
and dissimilar. The Cross is God's attempt to
break down the pride of man's own sufficiency.
And if you know the Lord Jesus Christ to be the
unique Son of God; and if you have entrusted your
life to Him and received from Him the blessings
which are in His gift alone to bestow; and if you
know Him to be God's Son in the uniqueness of
identity, then you will stand before His Cross with
awe, and then will " the blood of Christ, Who
through eternal spirit offered Himself without
blemish unto God, cleanse your conscience from
dead works to serve the living God." Repentance
is an act of our own wills: but the Cross gives to
repentance both its motive and its spiritual force.

It seems to me that in these ways the Cross becomes an intelligible method of salvation, even
though there be mysteries in it which we cannot
fathom. And I should like now to say to you what

I believe a reëmphasis on the Cross would do for
the world and the Church to-day.

The Cross is *the cure for spiritual subjectivism*.
We are living in an individualistic age, and individualism in religious experience always means
subjectivism. That is, we tend to attach undue
importance to the way we happen to think and
feel, and to be at the mercy of our states of mind.
For countless people to-day, religion is a vague
aspiration toward a higher life: more definite than
that they cannot be. They try to be fine, they take
a course of noble action which costs them something; and then because they do not find the satisfaction or success they think they deserve, their
religion goes into the discard. The Cross gives an
anchor to people like that. In an age of spiritual
flux, where great corporate authority is no longer
in force, we are bound to find our surest spiritual
authority in some life that is making a good fist
at the job of living: then one day we find a flaw
in that person, as in all other persons, and our
religion is reduced, or vanishes altogether, because
it stood in a personal loyalty, instead of in the
Cross of Christ. The Cross, by emphasizing God's
supreme part in our salvation, by offering us the
gift of it, a gift which we can receive but with the
creation of which we had nothing to do, gives
objectivity to our faith. The Cross is both an historic act, and an eternal process: it is the demon-
stration of God's part in our spiritual deliverance.
And this all means, in plain language, that when
your moods and your ideals and your human idols

go down, the Cross is a place to tie to. However you may feel, God does not change. Jesus on the Cross is the picture of God.

And the Cross is the *cure for over-emphasis upon human effort in religion.* We have of late been emphasizing how much we have to do in order to coöperate with God in what He tries to do for us. I am glad that there is surrender by which a man may take hold of conversion, that there is the listening attitude which we may adopt if we wish to know God's voice. It would be a sorry case if we could do nothing to forward the work of God in our lives. But when this is all said, it yet remains true that the very chief danger of the religion of our day is that our Christianity be only a creation of our own making, a disguised Humanism, with a thin veneer of Christian sentiment on the outside. There is a widespread notion that to be a Christian means using your will-power to live up to the ideals of Christ. Nothing is further from the truth. The heart of the Christian Gospel is not a human effort after moral self-improvement; it is the love of God in the Cross of Christ asking for response, and meeting that response with more grace given through the Holy Spirit. The heart of Christianity is relationship with God, not ethics— they follow. The pride of thinking that we can make ourselves worthy in God's sight is as great a sin as the pride of thinking that we may ignore God altogether. The deepest thing in the Christian religion is not anything that we can do for God, it is what God has already done for us. He has offered to us redemption, regeneration, a new nature, through the Cross of Christ. Our modern religion would be a far deeper and richer thing if we dwelt more upon that aspect of the Christian life.

Again, the Cross is *the only creator of genuine spiritual humility*. Protestantism has not been quite so successful as Catholicism in producing humility in its saints or in its believers generally. The individualism of Protestantism encourages independence, and independence encourages arrogance. I suspect that Catholicism produces humbler saints partly by its continuous emphasis upon the objective verities of the Christian faith, particularly the Cross. For humility is not a thing which can be cultivated directly. A man who tries to be humble may be as proud as Lucifer underneath: we all know of people who are proud of being humble. But genuine humility is a by-product,—a by-product, I suspect, of thankfulness. If you can make a man thankful for almost anything you have gone a long way toward making him humble. Now if anything is calculated to make men thankful it is the Cross: it gives us something we could not possibly achieve for ourselves. Dr. Glover says that the Cross was for St. Paul " a revelation of God's ways and of God's nature, so surprising in its inconceivable generosity that it melted his heart, and that, throughout his whole life, he could never think or speak of it without the element of wonder and surprise." Most assuredly, wonder and surprise make good parents for humility.

Let me bring this yet closer and more personally to you.

Do you wonder why you are not growing in the Christian life? I believe that it may be because there is not enough of the Cross in your experience. A friend of mine, to whom the Cross has recently become luminously significant, wrote me the other day, "For some time I have felt something lacking in me. I knew that I had been made very different by God, and that I had received help in my problems, that I had been guided by God, and had been able to help other people up to the point I had reached myself. I believed in Christ and believed that He had been the means of bringing the new life I had discovered. But I thought principally of growing toward God bit by bit, and did not see what I could claim from God as the fruits of the Atonement. I did not see what the new birth really meant." He then tells how his new realization of the Cross gave him a new release and spiritual power. Is it possible that you need by an act of faith to claim from God the full meaning of salvation through the Cross of Christ, instead of trying to develop yourself by your own spiritual devices?

Again, do you wonder why you have not got definite victory over sin in your life? We may have surrendered the sin over and over again, and on our knees given it to God. We may have used all the suggestions men could make to us, and yet there is no victory. Why? Maybe because we have not got the Cross as an experience. Our own wills are not enough: we need grace from the fountain of grace, help from outside of ourselves. When St. John called Jesus " the Lamb of God which taketh away the sin of the world," what do you think he meant? I think he meant just exactly what he said: that Jesus would abolish sin wherever He was accepted as a Saviour. Have you tried to lean, not upon the ideals of Christ, but upon the Cross of Christ, as a remedy for your sin? There is always the tension of self-effort in trying to defeat sin in our own strength. And there is always victory in relaxing that effort in favour of dependence upon the saving-power of Christ's Cross.

Again, Do you really love Christ? I ask you that very seriously. I don't mean do you love His principles, or His courage, or His influence in the world, or the outwardnesses of the Church which bears His name. I mean do you love Jesus Christ as a living Personality to-day? Do you know Him well enough to love Him? I do not mean now even relying on Him in times of need: I mean nothing less than personal attachment to the Living Christ to-day, not as an Ideal, but as a Person. Some of us will have to say in honesty that we do not. How, then, are we to begin? Only, I should think, by the realization of an infinite personal debt to Him. We love all noble characters in history in a sense: but if someone should throw himself into the ocean when we were drowning and drag us to safety, we should always hold that person in a place of particular devotion. We shall love Jesus

Christ when we see that this is exactly what He did: He did not die for general justice, but for you and me. He did not send forth from the Cross rays of grace and redemption so that they might be generally available: He sent them directly out to such people as you and me. If we can see redemption, not as a raft set in the sea of human need, upon which in company with countless others we can scramble out of our danger, but as a life-buoy flung out to us individually by Christ, we shall begin to see something of the heart of the infinitely personal Gospel of Christ.

Some of us here this morning are morally reformed through the ideals of Christ. We are not yet born again through the redemption of Christ. And that is no hair-splitting theological distinction: that is the difference between a religion which still centers in our wills, and one which centers in the Cross. We have thought that the greatest thing in religion was what we did to please God, whereas the greatest thing in religion really is what God did to save us. I ask you to test your whole religious life very seriously in the light of that distinction. I ask you to seek for yourself an experience of the Cross of Christ. It may begin in your own suffering, as your cross makes you realize the need for the light of Christ's Cross in which to interpret your sorrow. It may begin in a voluntary self-sacrifice which you know to be the only means by which you can break down resistance in another, as you see in this a faint shadow of what God was trying to effect in you through the Cross.

But it will only come fully when you realize in your innermost life that your salvation begins and ends at the Cross, when you crawl to Its foot in your sin, when you come under Its spell and let it break you and recreate you, and show you the nothingness of human righteousness and the infinite force and mercy of the love of God.

God in mercy strip us this day of the last vestiges of self-reliance, and help us to begin life anew trusting to nothing but His grace!

Let us pray:

ALMIGHTY GOD, HOLY FATHER, we come to stand before the Cross of Our Lord with awe. We try with our minds to understand, when it may be better for us simply to worship with our hearts. We pray this day to be released from dead works and from all trust in ourselves, that our consciences may be cleansed from them to serve Thee in spirit and in truth. The Cross is the medicine which we need. Heal us, Lord, and after the multitude of Thy mercies look upon us: through the merits and mediation of Thy blessed Son, Jesus Christ our Lord. Amen.

XII

THE FULLNESS OF FAITH

"For by grace ye are saved through faith: and that not of yourselves: it is the gift of God: not of works, lest any man should boast."—EPHESIANS 2: 8–9.

IN the preceding sermon we spoke of the central importance of the Cross of Christ in the faith and experience of a Christian. We said that what God did for us on the Cross is a fountain of inexhaustible blessing and power, and that faith in the Cross is the cure and corrective for the gospel of "self-help," so common to-day even amongst believers, which centers in the effort of the human will toward self-improvement.

To-day I should like to consider with you what faith in the Cross means, and what a fully developed faith should do for us.

The substance of faith in the Cross is found in our text: "For by grace ye are saved through faith: and that not of yourselves: it is the gift of God: not of works, lest any man should boast." It is the faith of Christians that the death of Jesus Christ revealed to us the heart of a holy and loving God, Who chose to suffer Himself for our sins rather than to inflict suffering upon us: and that by the perfection of the Sacrifice of Jesus we are saved, that is, we are lifted from the level of self-trust to that of grateful and abashed dependence upon the mercy of God. This thing was done, not only before we were born, but entirely outside the connivance of any human beings who ever lived. It was a transaction within the Godhead, between the Father and the Son, for the redemption of man. Unless you can give to the Cross a kind of awful objectivity, you will never understand its meaning for you. We are saved by what God does for us: " by grace ye are saved." I leave consideration of the further phrase " through faith " till later, for unless we understand the nature of grace, we shall never understand what quality of faith is needed to channel it to us.

By grace here, I take it that St. Paul meant *all* that God did for us through Christ and the Cross, and does still through the Holy Spirit. Grace, as it is found in the New Testament, means the spontaneous and undeserved mercy of God toward sinners whom, while yet in their sins, He invites to forgiveness and redemption. It always has in it whatever is the divine counterpart to the winsome human quality of " outgoingness "; it always means something beyond our due or rights, and it always implies an act of beauty, which causes joy in the hearts of those who are benefited, such an act as is faintly reflected in a piece of high and exquisite courtesy.

Grace is found all through the Gospel. The Gospel is like a piece of land well watered with streams of grace. You see it in the graciousness of Jesus toward women, children, the sick and the poor, in the beauty and benignity of all His ways. You see it in the open heart of His Father which He was always showing to men. But these streams of grace converged and shot out at the one great fountain of the Cross. It is here that we see and find grace abounding.

And it is this grace of the Cross which saves us. We did not make it, we cannot pay for it: we can only thankfully receive it. It is the gift of God. It is exactly as though a father should look out his runaway and renegade son, and offer him at once his whole patrimony and the run of his old home and the freedom of his father's love, if he would but accept the fullness of sonship as a conscious relation. The boy has not asked it, has not dared expect it, knows he has no earthly claim to it, may well have wished that he could elude his father altogether: but suddenly he is *confronted* with it, there is no question whether he may have to consider going back to his father some day—his father has already come out to meet him, has already offered him restoration and assumed his debts and forgiven his sins. The thing is not a possibility, it is a fact, and it becomes automatically an issue. Before there is any " ought-ness " in the Cross there is first of all this tremendous " is-ness." And Christianity which is to be powerful must ever begin in the declarative, not the imperative, mood.

To St. Paul and to all great experiencers and believers in the Cross, it has been a conviction that redemption has already been accomplished for mankind in the Cross of Christ, and that " to as many as received Him, to them gave He power to become the sons of God." It is a finished, perfected thing. There are no unfinished elements in it which God must complete in time, none which man can complete by acceptance, or leave incomplete through rejection. Like a perfect picture in a gallery, salvation waits to be enjoyed by those who will come to it: but whether they go, or whether they stay away, no more affects the reality of the objective fact of salvation than our absence from Dresden this minute affects Raphael's great Madonna. For St. Paul, who knew defeat and division as an unhappy Jew, Christ had filled all needs and satisfied all longings: and the heart of his experience of Christ was just here, that Christ did for him and in him precisely what he could not do for himself by striving in human strength to live up to the moral ideal of the Law. All effort to be good, and to rate standing before God, was as presumptuous as it was impossible. But the life and death of Christ had effected a reconciliation, in the power of which he stood, independent of any moral failures or successes on his part.

And clear down human history has come this faith in the objective validity of the Cross. We cannot create it by our acquiescence, nor destroy it through our denial. It is simply *there*, as immovable as a mountain of stone. There has been much controversy about the Cross: but this comes out of men's heads when they forget the experience of the Cross, and wrangle as to its explanation.

Nowhere is argument and debate so futile as here: more is likely to be given to one who simply stands in awe, before he begins to understand, than to any who comes saying he must first know all the theology of the matter. Faith in the unique saving power of the Cross is called by one great Scotch preacher to-day "the imperial vein of Christian experience." * And if you find this wrapped in a language you cannot fully sponsor, ask yourself first whether you know to what this inadequate language points. If you are made uncomfortable by old-fashioned phrases, and the vivid imagery of hymns like, "There is a fountain filled with blood," or other modes of expression which have in them figures of speech, which seem distasteful either to your æsthetic, or even to your moral, sensibilities, look behind them at what they seek to convey: that Christ alone made available a full redemption, of forgiveness, cleansing and restoration, for all men. And do not forget, either, that here is something which our cocky, impressionistic, modern Liberalism has lost, to its irreparable hurt. It was Goethe who said that the Church must ever turn to adjust her compass at the Cross. The Church has spent her life of late in every conceivable type of human sacrifice, much of which is wholly in the spirit of the Cross: but that is not the full meaning of the Cross, nor any substitute for it; it is in the category of "works."

We have not nearly exhausted all that needs to

* Dr. G. A. Johnston Ross: *The Cross: the Report of a Misgiving,* Fleming H. Revell.

be said of grace. But we must now consider the other part of the phrase: " by grace ye are saved through faith." It is not faith which saves us, but grace. This grace is not the creature of our faith, any more than the electricity in the wire is the creation of the wire: it only comes to us along the wire. So grace reaches us through faith. Now you will see here that the heart of our religion is in a very wise mixture of God's labour and ours. The redemption and the grace of the Cross were given us freely by God, and we could do nothing toward their creation: that rested with God alone. But the acceptance and appropriation of that redemption and grace come about through faith: and that rests with us alone. As I first looked at this verse, I wondered whether St. Paul meant that it was faith which is " not of yourselves: it is the gift of God." But this is not the right reading. He says that grace is the gift of God, but he does not say that faith is the gift of God. Faith is *our part* in the transaction, our part in the receiving of salvation. Let us never forget to tell men that their redemption stands in the Cross of Christ: but let us never forget to tell them also that the appropriation of redemption stands in their own choice and design.

What, then, is the nature of the faith which can channel the grace which saves? I suppose that for many of us faith has always seemed to mean an intellectual matter: it meant giving assent to one or all of the theological propositions inherent in the message of Jesus Christ: we have thought that we must weigh these with our minds, and accept or discard them, according to the dictates of reason. If we have gone a little farther we have begun to see that insight plays its part in faith, as well as reason: that our intuitions as well as our reason are to be employed in matters of faith, as they certainly are in all the practical concerns of life. Then we may have gone yet a step farther, and seen that faith is a kind of leap out toward God, in which the will also is involved: so that faith has become for us the function of the whole man, mind and heart and will: it is an attitude toward life and the Unseen in which all our powers are implicated. So strong is this faculty in full health, so filled with the power to recreate the life in which it is found resident, that it sometimes takes the central place in the Christian's life. We have many a time seen faith fairly create the things in which it believes: that is why it is called in Hebrews " the substance of things hoped for, the evidence of things not seen."

Yet I am convinced that we must go yet another stage beyond this. It appears to me that what we have just said of faith is all that human effort in the matter of faith can be expected to manage. The further stage of faith which I urge upon you is necessary, as I think, to meet the tremendous fact of Grace and the Cross of which we have been speaking. This calls for a kind of faith which has in it the very minimum of human effort, and the very maximum of receptivity. It wants no more human exertion than is involved in setting up a connection between the grace of God and our lives. The finest picture of this that I know is Michelangelo's Adam, in the Sistine Chapel, lifting up a languid finger to be touched into life by the finger of God. Let your faith be ever like that drooping, unenergized, but waiting and uplifted arm of Adam! I deliberately urge upon you to reduce the amount of effort you put into your faith, and to increase its consciously derivative and dependent quality. " When I am weak, then am I strong."

And then I urge you to go forward farther still, and to realize that such a derivative and dependent faith, having cast aside all hope in itself, may expect and receive of God such things as in its old and self-reliant form it could never hope to have! I am perfectly certain that all of us have weakened our faith by trying to inflate it with human effort, to make it strong through flinging our wills and personalities into it, as though it depended in the last analysis upon our somehow making it justify itself and come out all right. I am sure that this is a form of worshipping the creature more than the Creator, and of ultimately trusting ourselves as the final strength in our spiritual life. Do you not see yourself, your failures to go forward and to stand strong, as I say these things to you? I see myself all too clearly, and where I have sometimes put too much store by what I do in religion, and not enough by what God does.

Now I know that to some of you this sounds like a very advanced stage, and you are not in that advanced stage. Some of you still wonder about

God, and whether the vision of Jesus for the world was not too high, and whether we can ever be sure of these things anyway. My friend, one of the most glorious truths about this recognition of the Cross as the objective certainty of our redemption is precisely that it will wait for you until you can come up to it. The faith I mean can, I am sure, begin " yet a great way off," and God will see and encourage it. It may begin in your feeling only that some way in this baffling world of sad, suffering humanity, God suffered also. It may begin in your recognition of Jesus' nobility and rightness above His accusers and detractors, then and now, and God will honour it. You may have but an intuition that in the Cross God showed His heart to the world, and took the worst of the sting—its utter incomprehensibleness—out of evil: and God will look favourably upon that much faith. No man can have such a faith in the Cross as I am holding up to you to-day unless he believes first in the divine nature of Jesus: it is only as the Cross means God's own sacrifice that it has such stupendous virtue as to save men. It has been the sin of the Church many a time and oft to lay upon her people a theological demand which as yet neither their reason nor their experience can possibly endorse. But I believe that whether we be poor beginners in faith, or wealthy habitués of faith, we need to lift up our eyes from where we are, and see what the fullness of faith would really be.

A few nights ago I sat with a man who has been living a Christian life for years, but who has never

yet got a clean victory from sin and the fear of sin.
So representative is his situation, with his heart
right and fundamentally wanting to live as a Christian, and yet downed again and again by his gusts
of temptation and moodiness, that he may well
stand for many of us here this morning. I have
talked with him many and many a time, and I have
always before urged upon him that the way out lay
through a profounder surrender of himself. Surrender is merely faith active: it is the act by which
the desire of faith turns into determination, and
it has to be made before the forces of grace can
operate in any human life. But the oft-repeated
surrender of self to God, without a corresponding
increase in understanding how much God has already done for our redemption, is only flogging the
human will to greater activity. This time I said
nothing to him of further surrender. I said that
we had been putting our final trust in our own
faith, and not in God's grace: and we had got second things first. I urged upon him this time a full
recognition that God's redemption was available to
him whensoever he chose to appropriate it, and I
asked him to commit himself this time to nothing,
but only to accept in faith the great fact of salvation from God. I told him that I knew that if he
would make that act in faith, he would find himself not the possessor of, but possessed by, a Force
outside himself, greater than himself, independent
of his moods and his sudden seizures of temptation.
Again and again he came back, " But what if I fail
again? " And each time I said, " But when you

come to the Cross this way, you claim the power of Christ's redemption and His Holy Spirit. The connection has been made: you are no longer your own, you have no further responsibility than to make and preserve the connection. The crux of your spiritual problem from now on lies in daily, hourly re-appropriation of the power of the Cross." And then I said, " Will you kneel here with me, and claim as yours the full power of Christ's Cross, and trust Him to keep you, as you have not been able to keep yourself? " He said that he would, and he took that step.

Someone will say to me, "Ah, yes, but the test will come later." That is very true. It is one thing to ride for a few days or weeks in the splendid carriage of a new spiritual conviction, and quite another to stay in it and be borne along in it all our lives. I know no sinless Christians, though I know a few who fancy themselves to be such. " If we say that we have no sin, we deceive ourselves, and the truth is not in us." Yet we must complete the verse, " But if we confess our sins, God is faithful and just to forgive us our sins, and to cleanse us from *all unrighteousness*." The life of true victory in Christ must ever be the prayed-for and expected aim of every Christian's life. There is such a thing as a spiritual rebirth which carries with it an assurance of God's power to master sin for us, and which belongs in the realm of sheer spiritual miracle. So long as our last authority in religion is the word or encouragement of some other life, or the testimony of our fluctuating emo-

tions, we shall have our moral slippings and slid-
ings, our theological ins and outs, our spiritual ups
and downs.   But if we find the Cross as the
" power of God unto salvation," and plant our faith
there, and there claim the releasing power of the
Holy Spirit, we move up into another region than
the poor realm of our will-power, even when it is
buttressed by prayer and the helps of ordinary religious faith.   The life that finds this assurance is
twice-blest: once, in the joy and peace of the deliverance itself and then in the knowledge that it
has come " *by* grace *through* faith—not of ourselves—it is the gift of God."

  Recall for a moment the scene where a troubled
father brought a lunatic boy to the disciples, and
they could not cure him—they just did not believe
that a lad in his condition could be healed.   But
Jesus cured him.   And the disciples came to Jesus
apart, and asked Him, Why could not we cast him
out?   And Jesus said unto them, Because of your
unbelief: (insufficient faith, you see, was no faith
at all, but unbelief) for verily I say unto you, If
ye have faith as a grain of mustard seed, ye shall
say unto this mountain, Remove hence to yonder
place; and it shall remove; and nothing shall be
impossible unto you.

ALMIGHTY AND MOST MERCIFUL FATHER: We
thank Thee that our needs have been deeply dealt
with in the Cross of our Lord Jesus Christ.   And
we pray Thee for such an attitude toward His Sacrifice for us as may both enable us to understand

its meaning, and also to appropriate its grace through faith. We would kneel before the Cross this morning and claim for ourselves the forgiveness, the restoration, the power and the release of the Cross. And as the Cross is the seed sown in our nature, let Thy Holy Spirit come down as gracious rain to water it, that the harvest may be acceptable to Thee, Whom with the Son and the Holy Spirit we worship as one God world without end. Amen.